A Drop of Truth

THE AUTHORS

A & M Byrd are two authors who came together via a mutual friendship. Despite their transatlantic divide, they shared a growing disparaging view of what they saw as a subtle attack on civil human liberties, masked by a developing global pandemic situation.

Research took them down rabbit holes and the discoveries they unearthed led them towards a path of wanting to both help humanity and also to shed enlightenment on the dark and nefarious forces threatening to crush the planet.

Combining their writing, poetic and journalistic skills, they developed a story-telling technique that litters throughout the book, in the hope of offering a visual spotlight on the various, darker aspects of the situation of the past two years.

It is the wish of the authors, that the reader makes up their own mind and enters into their own rabbit holes of further research and discovery. The aim of the book is simply to enlighten. The rest is up to the reader so that they can choose to discern what they believe is the truth in world of untruths and hidden agendas.

A & M Byrd

A Drop of Truth

A
DROP
OF
TRUTH

The Awakenning Revolution

A&M BYRD

A Drop of Truth

This book is based on true events.

First publication in Great Britain as a paperback.
Copyright © A & M Byrd 2022
A & M Byrd asserts the moral right to
be identified as the author of this work under the
Copyright, Designs and Patents Act 1988.
A catalogue record for this book is available from the British Library
ISBN: 978-1-913949-18-1
Published in Great Britain
Distributed by
Writers Quill Ltd

'It is not famine, not earthquakes, not microbes, not cancer, but man himself who is man's greatest danger to man, for the simple reason that there is no adequate protection against psychic epidemics, which are infinitely more devastating than the worst of natural catastrophes.'

Carl Jung, The Symbolic Life

A Drop of Truth

Down The Rabbit Hole

A hare popped out of its warren. *Ah*! he thought as he looked up into the bright blue sky and stretched out the sleep from his body. *What a beautiful sunny day.* He smiled at a passing butterfly, who flirted with him and flitted above his head. He smiled at the buttercups and saluted the birds in the trees. Yes indeed, this was a glorious day to be alive.

He watched as another bunny popped out from a hole someplace to his right and behind him. Distracted, by the other hares arrival onto his perfect morning, he failed to look in front of him, until it was too late.

'Ouch!' he cried aloud. He shook his head and thumped his feet. What on earth did he walk into? Legs. Two long, thin pink legs attached to a large fluffy, feathery body. 'What on earth...?' he exclaimed as he jumped back to gain a better perspective. What he saw caused him both alarm and intrigue. The creature before him seemed to have lost his head, or at least had it stuck in the ground.

'Can I help you?' he asked gingerly as he approached the creature's neck, which was seemingly imbedded into the unearthed mound of green grass and dirt.

On hearing a voice from above, the creature pulled out her head and shook it violently. Her tiny ears were full of grit and soil. She blinked a few times from large, bulbous eyes with long elegant lashes covered in dirt. She made some spluttering sounds, opened her eyes wide, shook the remainder of dirt from her face and glanced around her.

The hare slowly shuffled backwards. This was not a creature he had encountered in the fields before and he wasn't sure if it had a penchant for eating rabbits. And with those long legs that were at least three times as high as him, this might not be a creature he could outrun. 'Hello?' he said in nervous trepidation.

The fluffy creature looked around her then stretched her neck down, so that her pointy, triangular shaped beak was almost nose to nose with his whiskers.

'I was hiding,' exclaimed the creature.

'Hiding? Why? From whom. Or what?' asked the hare sensing that this creature may not be a hare eater after all.

'From everything and everyone!,' she said and sat down on her fluffy bottom. Her legs seemed to disappear into her body.

'Really,' asked the hare moving closer, 'why?' The creature did not answer but instead, began to cry.

'There, there,' said the hare. "Don't cry. I'm sure we can sort this out and make things better,' he said as he soothed her with his words and stroked her feathers with his furry front foot. 'Er ... may I ask what kind of animal are you please?' he asked gently, causing the creature to stop crying.

The creature looked up and blinked a few times. She studied the curious creature before her and smiled.

'I'm an ostrich.'

'Wow. Never seen one of you before.' replied the hare in awe. ' So is that a thing of an ostrich; to hide their heads in the ground?' The ostrich thought for a moment before replying.

'Yes. It's what we do when we are looking after our eggs.'

'Oh, so you have eggs down there?' asked the hare looking into the hole left by the ostrich's head. The hole seemed empty and the hare stared back at the ostrich with puzzlement on his face.

'No I have no eggs,' declared the ostrich.

'Er ... Okay. So why *did* you hide your head then?'

'Because life is too complicated and I want it all to just go away!' cried the creature sobbing once again.

The hare was about to reply when she thought of something. She remembered the farmer in the field talking on his phone to someone about some crazy stuff happening in the human world. And a term the farmer continued to remain with him. The farmer said to whomever he was talking to, *Once you go down the rabbit hole of thinking, there's no turning back.'* At the time, the hare didn't understand, but when he repeated this to the Great Wise Hare who lived beyond the trees on the outskirts of the field, he was told that it was a term for truth seeking. The hare, who was a curious fellow, made it a point to listen carefully to the conversations of the Farmer and those who visited on a particular morning every second week. The men and women that gathered spoke about old systems falling, despicable, controllable elites and an evil plan to rule the world.

Since the Farmer's wife was a hefty woman who baked pies most days for the local market (on occasion rabbit pies), was always feeling the heat and thus always opened the window during these meetings. So the hare would position himself underneath the window and eavesdrop intently. It was far more exciting than the everyday talk of who had how many babies, field soil, weather and the carrot crops.

Perhaps he thought, *I can use the knowledge acquired from these meetings to help this ostrich, who surely was way out of her comfort zone as well as her habitual territory?*

'I have an idea,' he declared just above a whisper.

'Why are you whispering?' the ostrich asked. The hare looked around him. The nearby butterfly shrugged her shoulders and flew off. She never cared for this kind of talk. Sniff, nibble, fly and sunbathe was her thing. The birds were busy chirping and discussing this and that and he knew that the other hares were pre-occupied foraging food for their families.

'Tell me what you know,' said the hare in a conspiratorial tone.

The ostrich at first taken aback, then yielded to the strange, small furry creature before her. She told him of her fears and about a plan to inoculate the entire bird population from a terrible disease that threatened to destroy all types of flying creatures.

'They could kill us just to stop us from dying and apparently from becoming a danger to the human world!' she cried out in alarm.

She was about to sob once again and the hare could see her eyes darting around for the hole in which her head emerged from. It was her fears that were causing her to want to hide and those fears were creating an irrational response, though not completely without justification. Death and illness was a fear for all creatures, both large and small.

'You don't need a hole for your head, you need a rabbit hole,' he declared in triumph.

The ostrich stopped whimpering and stared quizzically at the hare.

'A what? Another hole? Made for rabbits? You have seen the size of me surely?' she declared raising her wide fluffy arms up and out from her sides. She almost knocked the hare off his feet in doing so, but he managed to hop out of the way.

'It's not a literal rabbit hole silly,' the hare said with jest, 'no, I am talking about truth and knowledge.'

'Truth and knowledge?' repeated the ostrich furrowing her brow.

'Yes. When you learn to decipher the difference between what is truth and what are lies, you gain more knowledge. And that knowledge leads to an awakening from a system designed to stop you finding out the truth and thus acquiring this knowledge. That's the rabbit hole. Once you start digging, the tunnels gets deeper and more twisted and more subterraneous than you could ever imagine.'

'Oh wow!' said the ostrich with wonder. ' And what use is having this knowledge? How can it help you in the end?'

'Ahh!' declared the hare with a knowing smile, 'then you have power. The very thing *they* don't want you to have. An awakened power of who you are and what you are capable of becoming.'

'Oh. And who are *they*?' the ostrich asked with piqued interest.

The hare smiled and he and the ostrich sat for many hours in the daylight sun talking and indeed going down many rabbit holes. When the sun was close to setting and both creatures had voices hoarse and tummies growling from lack of food, they said their farewells. Yet this wasn't then end. No, it was just the beginning.

WHILST YOU WERE SLEEPING ...

Whilst you were sleeping, they tiptoed on in, mangled your brain and stole stuff from within.

When your eyes were closed and your ears did not hear, they wrapped you in darkness and clothed you in fear.

Whilst you were sleeping, though your eyes still awake, your conscious awareness they did laughingly take.

When you were asleep though walking about, they told you don't yell, they said do not shout.

They masked your mouth, stuffed full your ears, silenced your brain and squashed compassionate tears.

Whilst you were sleeping, you didn't say no, as they silenced your loved ones, whom they said were your foe.

When wide asleep, as you nodded to them, they pilfered and squandered your freedoms again.

When you chose not to see and chose not to hear, your babes and children you didn't bring near.

Their hearts they did weaken and some lost their lives, but you chose not to notice, instead you closed your eyes.

Whilst fast asleep and watching the box, reading the news, your brain it was lost. You believed what they told you, believed what they said, can you be blamed for all that was spoken and said?

When you awaken and finally see, what kind of life will there be? Will your freedom be gone, like some fading sore bruise, will you be all alone because against friends did you choose? In a system designed to rule what you say, rule what you do and keep freewill at bay?

You gave up your health, you gave up your voice, you gave up your freedom and also your choice. You screamed for all others to follow the same and you cried out in blame as you screamed out their name.

You wore all your children as armoury tools, to protect your own health, as you listened to fools. Those who demand you do as they say, all thought of freewill, abandoned today.

So whilst you were sleeping and the darkness crept in, the dream catchers stole your light from within.

The giants who steal your children and feast, who laugh as you hand them their little hands and small feet. Those very same people who care not for you, for your mom or your nan, or your rock solid crew. They just want your allegiance, just want to control, they want you all sleeping, that you should know.

Whilst you were sleeping, when your eyes were closed tight, you did not defend and you chose not to fight.

WHERE WERE YOU THIS CHRISTMAS

They didn't cancel football and the EUROs went full ahead. Almost seventy thousand people were screaming off their heads. They played the games at Wimbledon, cosy seats they had a blast. That UK TV doctor, got away with smiling, beaming full on without a mask.

Ascot men and women with hats upon their heads, danced and hugged and glugged the fizz; social experiment they said. And what of those cars racing around the Goodwood tracks, where all squashed and watching punters sat happily back to back.

Granny sat alone for fear of catching 'it', whilst a virus with a moronic name floored millions in one hit. A sneeze and runny nose sent many to a test, which they failed and so they hid and Christmas did they miss.

No laughing turkey dinners, no cracker pulling hats, because the fear of God and a virus saw to that.

Where were you this Christmas? Were you sipping champagne toasts, snogging Ray from finance, or sparkling like the Queen of hosts? Or did they cancel Christmas, the office where you were work? Forced at home to type away, in slippers and housecoat? Did the planned year-long get together, with family you've not seen, or those life-long friends of yours, not go ahead it seemed? Someone got a test and then they couldn't come, scared because of granny or their lovely, shielding mum?

Everyone needs Christmas, from the lonely to the loved, to watching baby Jesus plays, to dancing in a club. From alcohol fuelled days, partying with your gang, to wrapping and unwrapping presents, until Auld Lang Syne was sung. To seeing granny in her paper hat, to grandad's funny jokes, to Mummy in the kitchen and Christmas jumper wearing blokes. To carving up a bird and stuffing full your tums, to watching Home Alone and all those Christmas movie runs.

They tried to cancel Christmas. They tried to make it stop, but Christmas lives inside us and thus it cannot flop. Christmas is a feeling — a time for love and joy. It cannot be created with just a wrapped up children's toy. It isn't a card to our neighbour, or a mince pie or candy cane, it isn't even dinner, for the family if they came.

Christmas is society, a communal time of year. And not one politician, scientist or rule, can cancel all that we hold dear.

So when the winter bites and darkness creeps on in, when pockets are rather empty and the bones of Christmas lay in the bin; remember to love on thy neighbour, to put on your party hat and live a life with a grateful heart, they cannot cancel that.

#MOCKINGJAY: Part 1 Chinese Whispers

High in the trees, one bird sings her song to the world. Others join in and soon the sky is ablaze with the musical harmonies of endless high pitched rhythm. Another bird's ears pricked up to a muffled but intriguing noise. He stopped his contribution to the group chorus and flew above the trees to investigate the origin of this new sound.

On the floor, beside a stream, sat a woman. At first, the bird thought the woman was crying. He was an elder bird, but with an inquisitive soul and he had seen humans cry many times before. However this human wasn't making the normal crying sounds or in a state of sadness as he has also seen them be when in despair. No, this one had her eyes closed and her face raised to the sky. The bird sat on a branch closer to the woman. He was mesmerised by her open trusting face. The sounds he heard from a distance was actually a chant and not cries. She was chanting and the melodious sounds from her lips soothed the bird whose head sprang from side to side as he listened intently.

One word came up more than any other. The Mockingbird, a natural mimic of sound, listened to the pitch of that one word that kept coming through the woman's lullaby chants *trust.*

'Trust,' repeated the bird, 'trust, trust, trust!'

The woman stopped her chanting and looked up. She was sure she heard the word *trust* reverberate around her. She got up and glanced around her, searching for another human. But for a moment there was just her, the stream and the sound of the birds singing somewhere deep in the forest to her left.

She was about to leave her place of quiet reflection and meditation; where moments ago, she had been praying for a miracle from her Creator to let her know she was seen. To let her know that she was heard; that her pleas for help and guidance in the midst of humanity's freefall had been listened to. Suddenly, from the trees where once the birds sang an unrecognisable tune of background melody, she heard a word. It sounded like *trust*. She stood breathlessly still in silence and strained her ears to hear.

'Trust. Trust. Trust.'

The word repeated over and over again ... *Trust* the word repeating through the trees and all around her.

For the longest time, the woman stood, tears soaking her face as she listened to the answer: a response to her prayers. Unbeknownst to her, a cheeky mockingbird had stolen a praying woman's word and passed it around the trees via other mimicking mockingbirds. She didn't know of this and instead, believed the word came direct from the sky. In that moment, she knew that she should follow her heart, trust in her Creator and pursue her mission. And thus, thanks to one mimicking mockingbird, the human race was saved.

THE STREAM

A man stood beside a stream. The summer day warmed his olive skin and in that precise moment, life was perfect. He sat on the cool grass and closed his eyes. The outdoor sounds of the gurgling stream and the chatter of nature, sent him into a sitting meditative sleep. And so he began to dream.

In his sleep, he dreamt he was sitting on a high ledge overlooking the world. God, a Being of bright white light, whom he sensed more than visualised, came and sat next to him. The man, felt comfortable and at ease with this Supreme Energy beside him, so much so, that he became inquisitive and began to ask questions.

'Hey there God,'(the name he called the Being of Light).

'Hello my son,' replied God.

'May I ask you a question?' The man turned to the Being of Light and squared him face on without fear or trepidation.

'Of course.' God's voice was warmth; loving and full of softness, yet also authoritative and definitive all at once.

The man, completely encapsulated by the beauty of the impression of a face, that was not actually a conventional face as such, sat for a moment in awe and wonder, before remembering indeed that there was a question he wanted to ask.

'Why is man so destructive?' he finally asked.

'Ah. Good question,' replied God with a slow nod and a smile. 'My son, when I created mankind, I did so out of love and nothing else. I loved man the same then as I do now.' The man contemplated God's words and perplexed by the non-answer, asked again.

'But why is man so intent on destroying that which you have created?'

'Who says that of man? Is that what you see? Is that what you think?' The Being of Light replied.

'Well yes! I mean look!' said the man as held out his hands depicting the creation of the world. 'You gave us all this and we war and kill and now there is a plan in place to destroy most of mankind for a few people's greed and need for ultimate supremacy. Therefore, man is destructive!' The man's passion tore at his heart and enraged his being. 'Why? I mean why?' he cried out in tears.

The Being of Light did not cry, or sigh or express sadness or remorse. Instead He simply sat and looked gently at the man. Then he placed his left hand on the man's right shoulder and smiled. Then in not more than a barely audible whisper, God said these words ...

'You are a father, right?'

'Yes. I have two young boys.' The man's face light-ened when he spoke of his sons.

'See! That's how I feel when I think of mankind. My face lights up and my heart brightens.' God leaned forward a little and peered into the man's soul. 'Do you love them even when they are outrageous, uncontrollable and disobedient?'

The man did not have to think.

'Yes of course. I love them always.'

'That's right,' laughed God aloud. 'You love them always. No matter what. And you know what that is?'

'Madness?' laughed the man mockingly. God laughed also.

'No my son. That is unconditional love. You love them no matter what. You made them and no matter what they do to either defy you or destroy themselves, you love them regardless.'

'Oh!' said the man with a shock of realisation. But then he thought a moment. 'But that does not explain why man is so destructive.'

'Do you force your children to do as you say or do you offer guidance and rules and hope that they have the good sense to follow what you ask of them?' God asked looking out wistfully to his created world.

'Well I can't force them or anyone to do anything. But I sure as heck hope they listen to me and follow my guidance and ... the man stopped in mid-sentence as he realised what God was inferring. 'Oh you mean, free will?'

God, the Being of Light, looked directly into the heart of the man and saw a pure soul with a pleasing heart of love, kindness and righteousness. The man felt seen. And in that one look he understood.

'So you created man, gave him all these wonderful things that exist in this world; companionship,

children, food, work, things and most of all a con-
science. And this ability to think means you gave
man free will to choose also. Am I right?'

God smiled and almost without perception, gave a
nod of his head. 'So man chooses to be destructive?'
the man declared in disbelief at the concept of making that choice.

'And man chooses also not to be,' God said with a
smile. 'Either way, it's free will and any decision he
makes, I'm going to love him anyway — unconditional love is just that; a love without condition. Just
like you have for your children.'

The man's train of thought ran into the path of so
many questions that his head started to ache. He
sighed, took in a deep breath and closed his eyes. So
many thoughts buzzing in his head. So many things
to ask God now he had His attention. He opened his
eyes and turned to face the Being of Light. But he was
alone, on the cold grass beside a flowing stream. He
sat for a few moments more watching the water ebb
and flow and noticed how in one place it hit the
rocks, yet kept going despite the obstacle; it simply
found a way around it.

Then he got up to head home and was hit by an
overwhelming urge to hug his loved ones and tell
them how much they meant to him.

'Unconditional love,' he declared just above a
whisper and his heart felt light and his soul felt good.

FOUR LEAF CLOVER

The little boy emerged from his rabbit hole dungeon, where darkness and terror and unspeakable ills were never to be spoken of again. He squinted and winced at the sudden exposure of light from the sun which though February dull and shrouded by a cloak of grey, stood bastioned in a longed for freedom sky of many moons and memories of not so long ago.

In the dungeon darkness of yesterdays, the boy might be granted to hear a hoarse whispering voice amongst some other's screams, which brought him back to a scene of otherness and dreams.

I remember the sky, one would say. Or *Can't wait to feel the rain*, one reminisced another dark, cave filled day. *I miss my mom*, whispered another, which sent them all into silent thought.

It made him smile, inward if nowhere else, though it was never a smile of happiness, or jest. It was simply a young boy who remembered what it was like to have a reason to smile. Like melting marshmallows round a campfire one long ago family holiday.

This lad, of barely twelve. Emerged into light from a darkened hell on earth pit. And breathed in the light of the wintery sun and thanked the Lord above, for he still believed, despite. Words of grace and kindness, that he had clung to, providing him hope when in reality, hope had abandoned most.

He breathed in sweet freedom and thanked his God and remembered words from a long ago spoken song, *Be still, for the power of the Lord, is moving in this place.* But Oh Lord, what a sad unearthly disgrace, did fall about this land, for his life to fall into those terrible, demonic hands.

The things that he had seen, a boy of not yet twelve, things he could not, forever un-see.

He blinked. The sun winked through the greying clouds, like an old man's beard, standing out from the clean-shaven men's crowd.

The things that he had seen, a boy of not yet twelve, who could not ever, no way, un-see.

He sighed. In front of the fluffed up sky and breathes. His lungs for months, clogged up with rotten, cave filled damp; cavernous pods where children lay, awaiting ill fate, day by day. Most would go and some new would come, but the cycle was always hum-de-bloody-hum-drum.

Screams and groans bounced off walls, echoing inside young minds' purposely vacuous halls. To survive you hide inside your head, or simply pretend those other kids were mercifully, quickly dead.

Tell-tales told of horror tales, of sucking of blood and rape, or stuff to make you pale. Of dissecting those who could not yet walk, and even those who hadn't learned yet to babble talk. Babies snatched from raped moms' wombs, horrific stories to make you weep with gloom.

And the boy who breathed in the rays of grey, who lived to tell an unhearing tale, sighed and exhaled out the pain. Not the pain for him, no, but then again, he has no words to properly explain the pain.

He lives. Though in rags and scarred from inside out. His voice but a croak, too much fear to shout; will he ever shout out, about the time inside? Inside those warren caves of sadistic torture? Will he regurgitate truths for his young comrades? Will he ever breathe a word, or will the world ignore him for a story quite too absurd? The people he had seen, from generals, priests and those you know, that would make you green.

But not with envy, maybe sick, because the world they have is abundantly crass and slick.

Idols gone, posters down, even someone dressed up with a crown. No more illusion inside his head, for all his dreams of one day, lay in tatters, torn, bloodied and horribly dead.

And yet he stands and breathes and thanks the very God whom he shouted at with mouth so vile, when the sweet young girl he met was dragged away and then defiled. And did not return with sweetness; she did not return at all. Another soul who was caught, trapped and tortured and then who took a ghastly fall.

The boy as he emerged, in a woozy state of perceived certain death, that he felt was just a matter of his time-allocated fate. He stood, face to the greyed out sun and thankful for each and every one, who came and set him free, to return perhaps to a momma's knee. And then he falls down onto his own; wretched, bloody, broken, dishevelled, half blinded and forever torn. And thanks he gave on that very spot, for he knew his blessings and he felt lack not.

Stolen in from a back route walk home; taken from his space by someone unknown. All the rest is one hellish blur, from one forced act of sodomy to another. *Do you hear?* And still, he kneels and praises God. For ultimately he feels he should. It wasn't God who tortured him, or made him scream and made him squirm. No. His momma taught him well, for he knew these beings had come from hell. All he had was his faith in good. And that someone from his own tough hood, would save his sorry little arse, from being ripped apart from those who are evil, mean and without one touch of human class.

And as he wept and thanked his God, his tear-drenched eyes saw something odd. For in the rubble of his bomb blasted jail, something glimmered, something green and pale. He blinked away the wet, his heart it leapt and jumped from fret. And gently plucking from broken ground, with a more than silent whispered sound, he cupped a treasure more than gold, one that he would memorise from now till old.

And what was in his blackened hands, of grime and dirt and blood soaked palms? A four leaf clover, oh so rare, and he could not help but simply stare. And then in eleven-year-old voice he said, 'A four leaf clover. Wow! I am indeed so blessed!'

Rock a Bye Baby

They are coming for your babies
the ones still in their cribs
They are coming for the elders too
so watch out for your kids

Seems they do not have a heart
they do not think of them
They have a big agenda
and love is not part of their plan

They'll drink the blood of babies
detach the kids from all their dreams
Light and hope and spirit love
is not part of the plan you see

So parents take up armour
and fight with all your might
It may be too late for you
but your kids still have their
freedom, right?

'Rock-a-bye baby, on the treetop.
When the wind blows, the cradle will rock.
When the bough breaks, the cradle will fall
And down will come baby, cradle and all.'

PIZZA ANYONE?

Look up pizzagate. Go on, go explore.
See what was delivered
behind hidden, closed doors.

A takeaway service not on your high street, for it's
merely for the rich and wealthy and globally elite.

If we said the word 'Epstein' or Saville perhaps,
would that make you question what they order,
these sick, twisted chaps?

One boy or two, a girl oh so sweet; she'll make a
neat pudding, a real succulent treat. A baby or tod-
dler with ole big Panda Eyes; oh my if you've
money, no end of such supplies.

But if you choose not to explore, this knowledge
that lies, right there at your door, before your
closed, unseeing eyes; we get it we do, being blind is
more safe. But shame we can't say safe to those kids
in that place ...

RING-A-RING O' ROSES

There may be something in the water, that's making us all quite weird. Or perhaps it's just the
weather, at it's really quite absurd.

My friends who once did love me, but who don't
think like me at all, got suckered into drama
spouted on TV.

They seem to have gone quite distant, for I'm not a
member of their club: I did not get injected at some
weird injection hub.

I wasn't invited to a party, or a wedding or to the
pub. Perhaps because I do not own a stamp that
says *Welcome to Our Club*?

But something's really strange, they're dropping
down like flies. Some are getting blood clots and
others, heart attacks and some just simply die.
It's never really known, the cause of all this pain,
but the story that I hear is the
same again and once again.

So I did a little research, for research's what I do.
And though I know you won't hear me, I hope two
words I found, could make you look too.

There's a toxic thing inside, the things they give to
us — in masks, and testing kits and swabs, and all
that disease preventing stuff.

It's called Graphene Oxide, a kinda friendly name I'd think, but when I did the research, I really had to blink.

In small doses it could be scary if ingested by us peeps, but in the high dose variety, it gave me real bad creeps.

For that apparent lifesaving stuff injected, with promises galore, of getting back to normal and getting out your door; is really just some damn poison that destroys inside of you, that plays a major part, in a sometime fall of you. Damn I so wish it wasn't true.

It's up to you of course, if you choose to take a look, to research these two words I mention, for I sure did take a look. And though I am no expert, I know this sure enough, that if someone really cared for you, they wouldn't pump you with this stuff.

Ring-a-ring o'roses,
A pocket full of posies,
A-tishoo! A-tishoo!
We all fall down.

THE JOKER STRIKES AGAIN

'What's that you're watching son?' The man asks his six-year-old boy as he enters in from doing stuff in the yard. His son, looks up from the couch and always happy to see his father, offers a huge smile and an explanation of the program on TV.

'Batman. It's a really cool episode Dad. You should come watch it with me,' the boy says hopefully as he shuffles on the sofa up to make room for his father to sit next to him. His dad was always so busy with work and other stuff and his two-year-old sister took up a lot of his parents' time. So he watched a lot of superhero cartoons and movies.

His dad sidles up next to him and puts his arm around him, which reminded the boy of when he was very little and his parents loved on him a lot more.

'So what's the story?' The man was a huge Batman fan and was secretly relieved to be doing kid stuff rather than big man things like de-weeding the yard; a job he really despised. But doing it was better than the nagging of his wife who in all fairness, had been nagging for over three months after he had promised and forgotten to do it many times over.

'Well, the Joker, is a bad guy. You know that right Dad?' the man laughed and nodded.

'Everyone knows the Joker's the baddie,' the man said with a shrug of his shoulders and a whiff of male camaraderie.

'Okay cool,' the boy said satisfied. 'So the Joker and this mad scientist guy have released a poisonous, green gas on the people of Gotham. It makes them cough and not be able to breathe properly and they have to go lie down to get better.'

'So it makes them real sick?' the man asked, adding, 'Do they die?'

'No they don't die. Some get real sick but most just feel sick. And cough. I think they are more *scared* of the green gas than anything really,' affirmed the boy.

'Yeah? Howzat work? The green gas is dead scary looking. No wonder they are scared,' he said wincing as he glanced at the screen. He watched as the ominous green gas poured out from air conditioning vents into buildings. The people of Gotham were horrified and screaming and running around to escape the gas.

'You missed the bit where the Joker and the mad scientist guy were talking before they released the gas.'

'Oh did I?' asked the man turning to glance at his boy. He watched in awe as the sun poured onto the boy's silken smooth skin and set his brown eyes alight and sparkling. In that moment, he loved his son more than life itself; more than anything. He tried to sound earnest as he said, 'what were they talking about?', but his heart was busting with love and joy. The boy didn't seem to notice and instead, reeled off the storyline to that point in the cartoon.

'So the Joker was telling the mad scientist guy that he wanted to control the people of Gotham, but that every plan was foiled by his arch enemy Batman,' the boy repeated looking to his dad to see if he was listening.

'Go Batman!' the man said with a mock victory fist. The boy smiled and rolled his eyes.

'Then the mad scientist guy gives the Joker this green stuff in a bottle. He tells him it isn't poisonous but that some people might get more sick than others. Just to scare them you know?'

'Yeah I know. Fear is the bad guys' calling card,' the dad said in a matter of fact way. The two nodded in affirmation and the boy continued.

'The mad scientist tells the Joker that after he releases the green gas, he has to then pretend to get ill with it himself. He must then go on TV and ask if someone has a cure. He makes out it's going to kill loads of people and without a cure, then everyone will die.'

'Yeah, that sounds like something the Joker would do,' said the father shaking his head. 'So what happened next?'

'Well, the mad scientist guy then gives the Joker a glass bottle of yellow stuff.'

'What's the yellow stuff?' the man asks the boy. He's totally hooked into the storyline now. He's wondering if he's seen this episode. It rings a bell, but then he's watched so many superhero cartoons in his lifetime, where the bad guy always has an 'invincible plan', that he could easily have watched this and forgotten.

'The cure!' the boy announces in a *Dun dun daaaa* tone.

'Ahhhh that old trick. Release the bad stuff that creates a problem, then offer the solution. Damn, that old trick's been around for centuries. I guess the old ones are the best hey boy?' the dad said nudging his son.

'I know right?' the boy said, delighted that him and his dad were sharing this connection. It was becoming rarer these days now Isabel was on the scene and both his parents were having to work. They both turned to watch the rest of the cartoon. The Joker was lurking in an alleyway with the mad scientist in tow. They were carrying the bottle of yellow stuff.

'What's he going to do with that?' the man asked genuinely interested.

'Ah Dad, you gotta watch!' the boy said in glee. He had already seen this episode and knew what was going to happen, but didn't want to let on. He really didn't want to end this moment with his father. He cuddled up closer to him and allowed a huge beaming smile to cover his face.

The two of them watched as the Joker and the scientist took to the stage with the Mayor of Gotham City. The police were all around them and cameras were flashing. You could see this was a matter of huge importance. Then the Joker announced to everyone that they no longer had to live in fear, because he and the mad scientist had discovered a cure for the strange new disease that threatened everyone. They no longer had to fear getting sick or worse because they would save the day.

Suddenly, Batman was seen watching from the rooftops. His laser eye computer beam (a new addition to his skill set it seemed), focused in on the yellow liquid in the glass bottle; the so-called 'cure'.

'Poison!' exclaimed Batman in shock. His laser beam eyes had deciphered the ingredients in the yellow liquid. An analysis was sent to Albert in the Bat Cave and within minutes a report was sent back to Batman via his computer watch. The yellow liquid wasn't a cure; it was a death liquid.

The father and son sat silent as they watched Batman fight the Joker and the mad scientist guy. Could Batman get the yellow liquid before it was released onto the people of Gotham City? It was tense watching and the man and the boy on the couch leant into each other, watching nervously; the fight could have gone either way. The Joker was cunning and determined and wanted to continue his evil plan no matter what. Batman meanwhile, was in a race against time and the people of Gotham were so filled with fear that they wouldn't listen to his imploring cautionary words to not drink the yellow medicine. As soon as Batman had managed to get hold of and dispose of one bottle of yellow stuff, the mad scientist guy was handing more out to the Joker. It was a desperate rush to stop two bad guys carrying out their evil plan.

'He'd better hurry it up!' said the Dad full of anxiety. 'If Batman doesn't do something quick, the Joker will get his evil way. And that's not going to look good for the people of Gotham City,' he said looking at his son and shrugging his shoulders.

'Don't worry Dad,' the boy said gently and reassuringly touching his father's arm, 'Batman always wins the day.'

The boy was right. Despite some very tense 'would he — wouldn't he?' moments, Batman defeated both the Joker and the mad scientist guy. The Mayor of Gotham City and the police, thanked Batman for once again saving the people and defeating the bad guys' evil plans. Meanwhile, the Joker and the mad scientist are bundled into a police vehicle and locked away until the next evil plan episode they are involved in.

'Phew!' said the man to his son with one last cuddle before heading off to finish the painfully monotonous de-weeding process before his wife and youngest returned from visiting his wife's sister. 'I really thought Batman wasn't going to pull that one off son!' The boy looked in shock at his father.

'Seriously Dad?'

'Well yeah,' replied the father matter-of-factly, 'I honestly thought the Joker was going to win.'

'No way! Batman always wins. There was no way Joker was going to defeat him.'

'Yeah I know Batman always wins, but this time, I really thought the Joker had him,' the man said scratching at his chin thoughtfully.

'Why do you say that Dad?' the boy asked furrowing his brow. He'd never heard his father question good versus evil in this way before.

'Well,' the man said slowly rising to leave his comfy seat, 'the people believed the Joker over Batman. Don't think I've ever seen that before.'

'Dad ...?' the boy asked in a curious tone, 'what would have happened if Batman hadn't won and the people kept believing the bad guys?'

'Hmm ... I don't think it would end well for the people son, do you? It's an evil plan after all. It's hardly going to be good for them now is it?'

'Dad?' the boy asked again calling his father back from exiting the door.

'Yes son?'

'Do superheroes really exist?'

The dad thought carefully for a moment. Then he put aside any adult doubts he carried internally and replied with a smile,

'Of course son. They are everywhere. You just can't see them.'

'Are you a superhero Dad?' the boy asked in wonder.

'Hah! We all are son, we all are.'

CYTOKINE STORM

There is a storm a 'coming
not like any other storm
for no heard thunder will be clapping,
nor torrential rain, to pour out upon the lands
Beware the storm that comes
with its hurricanes deep within
where flooding streams with dams and walls
escape routes blocking from our veins
A storm inside is brewing
the enemy wears black
silent soldiers releasing
molecules on cells as they attack

Stand fast with strong immunes
and do your job real proud
and silently please lift your voice
to defeat the cytokine storming crowd.

TEN GREEN BOTTLES

Eleven men started on a pitch,
Ready to play a game
The players, refs and all the fans
Stamped up to date that day.

One man fell to ground
Ten left on the pitch
Then a fan his heart just stopped
Ain't life a real sick bitch?

Two down and ten to play,
And then the ref he falls
Just collapses on the spot
No time to stop the ball.
In another stadium,
miles and far away
They had to stop the game you see
As they stretchered the midfielder far
away.

Another soul is lost
Someplace in the deepest State
A baseball player crumples,
Groans and then he meets his fate.

A cyclist, then a climber,
hockey players number two
Soccer players dropping down like flies
Did you see that too?

But hey, they're only bodies
Collapsing in mid play
No matter if they seem fit and strong

'Shit happens right?' The media seem to
say.

The fittest of the fit
Who train as the elite
Did not have time to say goodbye
As their bodies took a hit.

Maybe not ten bottles,
More like ten or twenty times or more,
Did start to play or do their thing
And then faced death's darkest door.

But no one bats an eyelid
No one questions why
These young and fit and healthy bods
Just stopped, collapsed and maybe died.

What was their thing in common?
What was the thing they had
That caused these guys and gals to fall
And made their future gone or bad?

It couldn't be that thing
They told us all to do
That wouldn't let them play their game
If they said no and made others blue.

No way you say in denial
That stuff would not to that
It must just be coincidence,
So let's leave it at just that ...

WHY ARE YOU TRYING TO HURT ME MOM?

'Goodnight my sugar. Sweet dreams. Mommy loves you very much.'

'Mommy?'

'Yes my love?'

'If you love me, why are you trying to hurt me?'

'What? I'm not! Don't be so silly. Why would you think I would want to do that?' Momma sits back in shock. She wasn't expecting that.

'But you made me wear a mask to school and they make me wear one all day long.'

'Not all day. You take it off sometimes. Besides, it's for your own good, to protect you and to protect others.' She sits up a little straighter.

'Then you kept me home and away from all my friends and wouldn't let me go to the park or do sports, or even see Grandpappy. And now Grand-pappy is dead and I have no one to take me fishing.' The boy looks sad and confused.

'But honey. It was the rules. And we did it to keep you safe and to keep Grandpappy safe from catching the disease.'

'But he died anyway and he died alone without anyone holding his hand and making him feel better. Why would you not let me say goodbye to Grand-pappy? I needed to let him know he was going to be okay because there are big lakes in heaven and he could go fishing up there. I needed to remind him not to be scared and to hold his hand. But you wouldn't let me go.' The boy was tearful and angry now.

'Listen son, Grandpappy was old and he must have caught it when he went to the shops, or when he fell down and hurt his leg and had to go to the hospital for treatment. I miss Grandpappy too and we couldn't go see him because those were the rules.'

'But I don't understand how he got sick if he only hurt his leg? He didn't go to the shops because Aunty Jenna got his shopping delivered. You told him not to go to the shops remember?'

The momma sat fearful. Her son's words cut through her. Why was he being like this? She missed her father too, but they had to follow the rules. What was that thing about heaven?

'Who told you that there were lakes in heaven?'

'Grandpappy did. He told me a lot of things. He told me all about God and Jesus and heaven and angels and how there was so much beauty all around us is we opened up our eyes to see it. And now he's gone and everything feels darker. It's not fair.' The boy sobs. Momma comforts him but she feels removed from his pain. She doesn't fully understand the source of these deep emotions.

'Well then I am sure Grandpappy is fishing on a big lake somewhere in heaven and that Grandma is bringing him a mug of cocoa like she always did.' The momma felt assured that her appeasing words would at last comfort him and that she could leave his room as he fell asleep. She still had things to do downstairs and it was almost time for her favourite program on TV.

'So why are you trying to hurt me?'

'Whaaa?' This outburst brought indignant rage to the mother's chest. How dare he accuse her of this after all she has done for him! 'Don't be so silly and go to sleep!' she replies curtly.

'No! I want to know why?' he cries out.

She frantically searches her son's face for clues, then finally says, 'Why would you say that to me son?'

'Because the masks don't let me breathe. I now have a cough and that cough makes the other children laugh at me and call me Covid Cough. I have spots on my face where my skin feels like I am suffocating it with my foul breathe, which I can smell all the time. Please stop giving me garlic. I keep throwing up in the bathroom after lunch because I hate the smell in my mask.'

'I'm sorry,' says the mom confused, 'I didn't know. I was just following the rules because I want to protect you and protect others.'

'And we have to stand away from each other all the time and can only play with the same people in bubbles. Brett in my bubble, is always hitting me and stealing my food and if I tell the teacher she says we have to get on because those are our bubble friends and that's that. I hate how Brett makes me feel at school. I sometimes hide in the toilet or make myself throw up so I don't have to be in the bubble at play-time or lunch.'

Momma is shocked. Her son being bullied and making himself sick? 'I'm sorry,' she said, 'Perhaps I can talk to Miss. O'Brien after school tomorrow?'

'No! Brett will hate on me even more. He picked on another boy in our bubble and then started beating him up after school because the boy's mom told the teacher on him.'

'Maybe I can speak to Brett's mom?'

'No! She's the reason he's like that because his pop hits her and Brett. I heard Luna tell Amy yesterday.'

The mom sat back and thought for a moment.

'We will sort this out I promise. We can't have another boy make you sad to go to school. I hate seeing you so unhappy.'

'Mom you don't get it do you? I'm unhappy because I feel like I have lost my old life. We wash our hands all day long and I now have red raw hands because the soap is so stingy. We wear masks that gives me coughs and spots. We can't hold hands, or hug, or play contact sports, or ever touch anyone. We are freezing in the classrooms because the windows are open all day and I never see any of my other friends in any of the other classes. I miss seeing Grandma, but am glad she died before this horrible virus was here, because she would feel so lonely and I would feel so sad for her all the time. I miss Grandpappy so much my heart hurts when I say his name or think about him. I never see Dad because he lives in Australia and he can't visit and he was only meant to be there for a few months. I can't go play with friends in the park or have sleepovers, or go to big parties, or go swimming, or ice skating, or bowling. I hate it. I hate my life!'

'I'm so sorry baby. I really am.' She stoked his arm and soothed his forehead as she always did. Then she lightened her face and smiled.

'We'll soon be back to normal now we are all getting the vaccine! I had mine and it'll be your turn soon. Then before you know it, everything will be okay and completely back to a new kind of normal!' She said with a chirpy grin as she regurgitated words from the media that had comforted her when she once felt so fearful.

Her son did not smile. He did not lighten up his face to match her own. He did not allow words to bounce around the walls like hers had, in order to soothe the feelings of rage and confusion held deep within.

'You don't get it do you Mom? They told us at school that we will probably have to wear the mask for a very long time. Still stay in bubbles and socially distant and keep washing our hands with that horrible soap, even IF we all have the shot!'

He looks up at her, tears flowing without restraint down his cheeks. His mother, not knowing what to say or how to appease her crying, anxious child, simply sits and wells up with tears herself. He was right, it didn't make sense; it wasn't fair. But rules were rules and if that's what they were being told to do then that's what they should do. She trusted the science after all. They knew what they were talking about didn't they? Didn't they?

'It'll all be okay darling. It'll soon be back to the way it was. Once we all protect ourselves and each other from this dreadful virus, everything will be fine.'

'Will it Mom? Will it really?' he asked with such a deep, resigned sigh and a look so solemn that even his grandpappy fishing on a lake high above the clouds stopped to listen, 'You are my mom and I know you love me and want the best for me, but Mom, why are not stopping them from hurting me?'

MASKING

Where have you gone? The who that was you? The one who listened to that fella from WHO; who said don't wear one then said wear three, blimey he's a contradiction in terms isn't he?

Babies they grimace for not learning to smile, for masked faces are all he/she sees walking by. Kids are confused, teens are much worse and convinced that the world carries walking dead like a hearse.

The fearful hide behind colours of cloth, that do little else but make them feel good and could hide a cough. But alas their insides are not as bland as their face; for their lungs are compromised, aggrieved and displaced.

But hey, if it makes one feel good and a real decent guy, then why would you remove it, why would you try?

It's a habit you've formed for it takes just four weeks and the fear and the guilt could make you feel weak. That you aren't ticking that box that says *good little soul* for masking your face and hiding that hole ... in your mouth where your voice might just lie, but why would you voice that? Why would you try?

The powers that lead do not want that one voice, or that protest or questioning over your rights or your choice. They want complicit nations that subject and bow down and they really don't want, to see the face of the clown. The one who talks out, who laughs or will sing. Blimey don't do that or they'll be imprisoning ... you and your mates who also talk out, who question and argue and protest and shout. That the world has gone mad and people seem to have lost, their individual character that we adhered to the most.

But there may be another reason for us to wear those damn masks — it enslaves us to a master, acquiescent to host. We bow our heads in silence, we mask our mouths in fear and we do not allow another soul to touch us, or come near. Have we lost our sense of family, of a community and hub? Have we silently resigned our space to live without any social club? A club where people sing and dance and hug, and laugh and smile; what happened to that happy place, from which we've run a mile?

Just A Face Accessory

Do you feel safer and always unseen
behind that cloth of
bright coloured green?
does it hide all your spots
that have suddenly come?
and does it mean that you're saved
from a smile at a strange someone?
you can curse all you like
with your mouth now a'masked
and your grimace and anger
is no longer classed.
Oh freedom has come
from not being exposed
yes, you're a face-less mean person
individuality closed.

FITTING IN

If I took it, had it, got it, then I wouldn't be watching you, get it, take it, have it and feel the way I do.
Double, triple jabbed and feeling fine.
Let into big events, drinking wine,
in fancy tents.

Bowls of strawberries on Centre Court
Ascot Hat on as you cavort,
with all the other willing peeps
blind to truth and choose to sleep.

Whilst I ... I, I sigh.
On the bank, as I watch you swim,
joining all the fish with no thought or whim.
Whilst I do not jump in,
not because I cannot swim,
but simply because I know the state,
of the water and thus our fate.

But oh, for just one moment so,
I would like for me not to know,
what I do know from being awake
and thus the dreaded stuff I just cannot take.

WHY?

Can you not see what we see?
Feel what we feel when we feel what we feel?
When we see through the veil
they wrapped us all in,
slowly, like a slow snail's slimy trail.

Sneakily they encroached
on our freedoms and laughed, as they broke
the social bond of glue once so strong
of moral rights that kept us from praising wrong.

But alas,

like a thief at night in clothes of dark
swift and slick as a predator shark.
It came — they came — then stole,
the truth wrapped moral code
of one and all.

And soon you handed on a plate
yours, and ours and mankind's fate.
For you did not stop to ask them why!
No, you didn't even try
to stop and ask.
Why did you not stop and ask them why?

And those who do are excluded and blue.
And as for you, why did you not also ask the question?

And instead let the elite decide mankind's destination?

THE FISHING TRIP

'Hey Dad, can I ask you a question?' Paul asked, watching the old man sip on his freshly made coffee, the boat bobbing gently on the water. It was one of those gloriously sunny days of uninterrupted blanket blue, with the water silent and calm, save for the slight *glup* sound of the water hitting the boat. Perfect day for fishing.

'Sure son,' the old guy replied glancing over and squinting as the sun hit his vision. He noticed that his oldest son was struggling to form the words in his mind before expelling them out. He had been watching him do the same thing since his first words as an almost two year old, thirty-four-years previous. He noticed he was taking his time to form the question. Something big was coming.

Paul looked directly at his father's profile since the old guy had returned to studying the water. 'Tell me what happened during the pandemic of 2020 to 2022.'

The old guy sighed. It was a conversation that had to happen someday, but he had been dreading it. He guessed today was as good a day as any.

'What specifically do you want to know son?' he asked turning to look directly at his son.

'Everything I guess. I mean ... how could it have happened? I've been thinking a lot about it since Josh came home from school saying they had been learning about it. I think the topic was something about cognitive dissonance. I looked it up and am pretty confused how a whole planet of people believed the lie you know? I mean, it's been compared to the Nazi regime a hundred years or so previous, but this was the whole damn world!' The younger man looked shocked and shook his head. 'I thought you might be able to shed some light on it?'

Silence sat between the two men for a few moments. The older guy opened a drawer in the filing cabinet of his memory. It had been a long time since he rummaged in there. He pulled out files and flicked through mental notes. It was all in there; all the answers to Paul's questions. However, it was a drawer that he kept under lock and key and hadn't ever wanted to open again. He took a big sigh and started to explain as best he could.

'Well, it was a long time ago, you know? You were just a few years old at the time.'

'I was three in 2021,' Paul interjected.

'Yes, that's right. Scary time as a parent I can tell you. Being awakened and aware of what was really going on and watching all these people around you falling for the lies and deceit and seeing them not understand why you didn't want to be a part of it; didn't want the *thing*, you know?' he glanced at his son for understanding.

'You mean the jab?'

'Yes. Exactly. The poison. First it was one jab, then two, then three, then it went on and on until the Big Exposure. By then, it was too late for so many ...' the old man's mind wandered off as he remembered all those he had lost. His parents, grandparents, brothers, their wives, one of their children, friends and their families. The list went on and on in his mind like a scroll unravelling into the sea. He heard Paul clear his throat, bringing him back into the present.

'I know this is a bit painful Dad. I guess that's why I never asked either you or Mom before.'

'I promised your mother I would leave it all behind. It's such a heavy weight to carry. She suffered terribly afterwards. She was always anxious, you know that. But this ... this was an awful time for her. So often she wanted to give in.'

'Didn't she have the first dose?' Paul asked.

'Yes she did. But she had a terrible reaction. Bell's Palsy on her left side and years of awful skin flare ups and joint swellings. Then there were the shakes ... she was never the same again. Poor Esther,' the old man said, his eyes clouding with watery memories from tapping into the hidden vein of a deep stream of pain and heartache.

'Sorry Dad. I know how much you loved her. I miss her too,' Paul replied, his voice paling away.

The old man cleared his throat and continued with his story. 'It started with just a few weeks to *flatten the curve* they said. Lockdowns took over the world. Then the masks and the social distancing came. Weeks turned into months. Everyone lived in perpetual fear and somehow, strangers, neighbours, friends and even family, became potential virus spreaders. Social contact was avoided at all costs. Some people were so fearful, they even crossed roads or avoided eye contact with others. People stayed home, stayed away from each other and some went insane in the process.'

'But surely they must have noticed the inconsistencies in the narrative being dished out by their governments, leaders and the media? Looking back it is *so* obvious that they were making things up as they went along, or simply telling untruths? That's the bit I don't get Dad. Why did so many millions of reasonable minded people go along with it? It baffles me.'

'Yup. I agree with you. It baffled and confused the hell out of me at the time too. Looking back, I can see the correlation between what happened with the Nazis and Germany and what happened during that pandemic. Like Josh and all the kids are being taught at school now about those crazy three years in the early 2020s, so we were taught about the mindset of people in Germany who accepted and went along with what Hitler and the Nazis spouted out about the Jews and other ethnic minorities at the time. The Nazis convinced the German people that what they were saying was the truth. They coerced them into their way of thinking. It was the same during the pandemic. The same coercion tactics of guilt and fear were used to convince the people back then.'

The old guy sighed and drained his mug. He sat back and stared out at the water, lost in the waves of memories. His mind floating between Nazi Germany and the Covid-19 hysteria. He was silent as he shook his head in disbelief.

'That's the part that I don't get Dad. Surely the people of the time would have recognised the signs? I mean history repeated itself and there were clues left behind right? Why couldn't they see what was happening?'

The old man looked squarely at his son's troubled face. He remembered then that the boy missed out on so much, but since he was so young during that time, he didn't know that his upbringing was not the norm. That people dying around him, food and fuel shortages, constant threats of violence and wars and global instability; bouts of no schooling and no hot water, heating or electricity, were not what life was meant to offer a three or four-year- old. Life was so different for him and his brother than it was for those who enjoyed childhoods before him in the same social situation.

'Truth is son, that we were constantly bombarded with the same messages of fear and lack of hope and that the jab was the only cure and that the next jab would do the trick, and the next and the next and so on. They threw strange sounding variants at us and told us how dangerous they were. The only solution they said, was to get the shot, to protect others so we could protect ourselves and therefore keep protect-ing others. If you didn't take the shot, you were la-belled 'anti-vaxxers' and selfish and the reason for us all not getting *back to normal*.

In truth son, it was a big lie. But when you are constantly seeing or hearing the same message over and over, it's so hard not to believe it. And so many did. I guess they didn't want to *not* believe it.'

'That's cognitive dissonance right? To go along with a belief or thought because you don't want to hear anything conflicting? Am I getting that right?' Paul asked opening his lunch box. His stomach had been rumbling angrily, a reminder that it was way past lunchtime.

'Yeah that's kinda it. Being fed one message by politicians and media globally and being told to ignore all other contradictory information. It confused many, but the majority went along with it. It was so easy to convince them that their way was the truth and the only path they should take and that all other information was fake or disinformation.'

The old guy shook his head in disbelief as he remembered days he chose a long time ago to forget.

'Why not you Dad? Why didn't you believe it? What made you different?'

'Good question son. Good question,' the old man replied with animation. He got up from his chair and stretched. He placed both hands on the side of the boat and looked down into the water. There was more movement in the sea, created by a light, easterly wind. The words he spoke next were more to the sea and the sky than to his questioning son.

'I've been wondering that for the longest of time Paul. Back then, I just felt instinctively that I had to wait and watch. Call it intuition if you like, but I just *knew* that something was wrong. I told your mother that we should wait until March, 2022, when we had a full on winter. I reasoned that we would know how effective these so-called *vaccines* were by then. If I saw the benefits of taking it by that springtime, then I would roll up my sleeve and get it. Simple!'

'So you didn't take it because you followed your instincts?'

'Yeah, I guess. I was also quite spiritually minded back then. I saw through the whole religion Church thing a few years back after my own mom got let down by people in her prayer group. I guess that experience made me step away from organised religion. I didn't stop believing in a higher power, God, Source, or whatever it is, but I wasn't what you'd call 'religious.' I guess you could say I was tapped in to Source and that gave me more freedom to trust myself more. I dunno; it's so hard to explain.'

The two men were silent as they both contemplated the words that still sat in the air between them. One was digesting concepts and opening pages of a book just handed to him; the other was lost in a mental movie of a long ago time.

'What about Mom? Did she feel the same?' Paul asked, breaking the silence.

'Yes and no. She shared the same spiritual freedom as me, but was less politically minded. I was a bit of a rebel thinker back in those days,' the old man said with a wink and a knowing smile. 'Your mom ...

well, she was far more conformist. If she wasn't married to me, she'd have gone along with it unquestioning. When she got the first jab, it was because of her thyroid dysfunction and her low immune threshold due to a severe bout of glandular fever as a child. Although I told her to wait, her doctor convinced her she should get it to protect her. I guess like most people, she was fearful. She didn't want to catch the virus, since she believed she was immune compromised. Thing is son,' he said turning square on to face the younger man, 'they did a real good job of convincing you that you were in real danger if you didn't take it. And it was worse still if you had any kind of illness, disease or type of immune deficiency. The very people who needed to retain a strong immune system, were the very people they first targeted to get the shot. The old, the sick, the vulnerable. Damn them for being so darn heartless.'

'Poor mom. She did what she thought was best I guess?'

'Yeah but it made her health so much worse after that. And then a few years later she got cancer. It tore through her within eighteen months. Her doctor said her immune system was too compromised to fight it. We'll never know for sure, but ...' Paul watched as his father screwed up his face with anger and resentment. He walked over and touched his father's hand which was still on the edge of the side. The old man closed his eyes and his son watched as a tear fell from his left eye and rolled off the cliff of first his cheek, and then his chin.

'I'm so sorry Dad. Mom had the best smile. And the best hugs.'

'Yes son, she certainly did,' the old man said placing his right hand on his son's left arm. 'She loved you both so much. It pained her to leave.'

The two men stood silently abandoned to their thoughts of a woman they loved but lost many years previous. Paul felt the wind picking up and knew it would soon be time to head back. Eloise his wife, was expecting their catch for supper tonight and he had more than enough for a few meals in the cool box.

'Dad, one more question ...?'

'Sure son, ask away.'

'What made them stop? Why did it end suddenly in 2022? We learned all about their one world government plan, the Great Reset and the plan to annihilate so many of humanity. I mean, it was disgusting and unbelievable, but, then one day they just stopped and the world got to recover. Or at least those of us who were left did anyway. What really happened?'

The old man stopped looking out to sea, let go of the pain and sadness that still crushed his heart decades later, and turned to look lovingly into the face of his boy. He saw the fine lines, the slightly receding hairline and the encroachment of grey peppering his wavy dark hair. And in that moment, his sadness dissipated entirely as his heart was filled with love and hope for his child and his young family. Then, with a smile spreading knowingly across his face, he simply stated,

'We won. We won son, we won.'

#MOCKINGJAY: Part 2 The Forest

The sun poured through the kitchen window, re-fracting light onto every light reflecting surface. The silver colander drying on the sink, the half-filled water glass beside her resting hand; the cutlery on her plate, left discarded from the night before.

She closed her eyes and drank in the early morning warmth that permeated through the pane. She breathed in and gave thanks internally. Despite what she knew, it was a good day to be alive. She opened her eyes, adjusted to the world that was her reality and turned towards the door, collecting her bag and the tools of an archer. Her cat meowed and purred at her feet, meandering in and out of her legs. She smiled at his futile attempts to lure her to a lazy morning accompanying him on the sofa.

'Laters Archie,' she purred back, touching the tip of his tail.

'Meow.' He wasn't impressed. But then she never was the type of owner to simply sit beside her pet, be absorbed by the box and do nothing. After two years of living with her, he should know that by now, yet still he asked. Every morning they went through the same routine. One day she would give in, he was sure of it.

However, this morning, resigned by her determination to not comply with his demands to be sofa stroked, he lifted up his tail and turned on his feet. And out she walked. The click of the door causing him to turn back and stare wistfully for a long time after he had heard the vehicle pull away.

Sofia drove absently. Her hands and body knew exactly where they were steering her, but her mind was full of dreams and visions. She wasn't just awake; she was being called. There was a mission; she felt it so strongly, that her every waking moment lapsed into the conditioning of these thoughts. The word *trust* singing through the trees was the confirmation she needed. The more she felt it, the more information came to her.

The awakening of just one year ago, was being speeded up the past two months at an incredible rate. She couldn't define it; describe it or even speak about it. She simply knew that her time to act was soon.

How could she have been asleep for so long? When life had thrown her so many challenges and lessons and the times that she thought she wasn't going to make it out alive. Yet here she was. Alone save for her not-so-dumb, crazy cat. Everyone else she trusted, knew and once loved, had succumbed. She wasn't alone, she knew this, but she needed to be alone right now.

When they came for the children, she knew she had to leave the city. She took a sabbatical, which truthfully, her employer was pleased about.

Relieved more like since she wasn't complying and creating a scene in the process. They couldn't dismiss her as she knew her common law rights. She also had a great lawyer contact who was also wide awake. So they jumped at her offer to take a year out 'for educational development' and even offered to pay her, including a hefty bonus; 'guilt payment' she called it. She didn't complain.

Billy had succumbed and the existing emotional distance between them simply grew into an unreachable canyon. So no boyfriend to tie her down. She was an orphan and an only child, so no emotional family ties to consider either. Friends fell off friendship cliffs, like one crazy lemming after another. Acquaintances were just that. She had nowhere she had to be and no-one she had to be there with.

She parked her truck up at the same spot she parked every day without fail. No wind was too harsh, no sun too burning and no rain too wet. This had been her calling for weeks and she was simply responding the only way she knew — through her instinct. And her gut right now was screaming that soon the waiting would be over; soon the mission would be disclosed and her part in it revealed.

She grabbed her bag filled with essentials including a water bottle, snacks and a packed sandwich. Same every day. Routine right now was key to walking this designated path. Alongside the bag, she picked up her bow and arrow.

As she walked along the bank beside the stream and then into the forest, she tried not to allow her mind to focus on the negative thoughts that barraged her soul daily. The knowledge and truth that had been revealed to her the past few months were a constant threat to the lightness of being that was crucial for retaining a healthy mind and thus her mental survival. How could she pretend that all was well, when she knew of the darkness descending on humanity? That's why she had to get out. Those millions of people around the world falling under the wicked spell of a demonic few. How could a few thousand hoodwink billions of people? How was that possible? The more she thought of it the darker she felt, so she tried not think: it was much easier that way.

She could just about cope when Billy succumbed as she had already started to doubt the authenticity of his professed love of her. The affair was less of a surprise than his decision to get the shot. He had always been so anti-government and propaganda; anti-war and all about peace, freedom of choice and expression, and always slightly off centre of normal day-to-day life. As soon as he had the second dose, he changed. Literally overnight. He no longer saw what was so obviously blatant before. His version of truth and integrity became the version told by the professed leaders of the world. He spoke the words of the narrative, regurgitating the same untruths and fear daily. Perhaps she pushed him towards the girl in the auditing department of his office, because she wanted an easier way out than to simply say,

'we've lost that thing that once made us great. We no longer think the same; we no longer have that connection Billy. I'm sorry, but it's over.'

Instead, she chicken shitted it and allowed him to walk away. 'Pah! It's easier,' she said aloud, caught up in the memory of the final weeks with the man whom she had believed she would one day marry.

Her feet scrunched their way along the dried out leaves descended from the canopy of trees above her. Fall was encroaching its whispery shadows on the late summer days. Fall always filled her with a sense of loss. Even the very word 'Fall' filled her with melancholy of what was once in existence and what was to come. It wasn't just the leaves from the trees that would soon come crashing down.

Humanity was in extreme danger and blindly losing the war imposed on them by the subtle campaign of the self-proclaimed victors. Despite that victory being premature and unfounded, it still permeated her heart and filled her mouth with distasteful bile. She shuddered at the thought that threatened always, to crush her, just as her boots did to the decaying ground she walked upon.

She saw her spot and stopped. An hour had passed and it was already close to eleven in the morning. She unpacked the drink from her bag and took a large gulp. She sighed and stood with eyes closed as she breathed in the forest air. Her ears attuned into the woodland sounds. Birds of many species, rustling rodents, insects in stridulation, the wind teasing the leaves and branches into a whispering hush and the other animals that sneaked around, whilst busying themselves with their daily lives.

She pulled out her bow and arrow. She lived from the land and one rabbit could feed her for a week. Yet it wasn't about the kill. Her mission wasn't about this type of prey. Mankind was the prey of a select few hell bent on torturing the masses with fear and insecurity; constantly changing the rules and throwing the unthinking into confusion and fear. Being awake, she watched incredulously at how easy it had been. Centuries of freedoms fought, lost and won, only to be handed over with open arms by an unseeing, blindly accepting human adult majority. The planning that must have gone into this refined level of psych ops was astonishing. Damn it for being so easy for them.

She lifted her bow, placed the arrow in place and focused. She stood without the sound of breath, statuesque still and waiting. Ears pricked for the one sound she hoped to hear. Ten minutes or so went by and still she waited with composed anticipation. Suddenly, a small movement from the right of her, caught her eye. She held her breath and steadied her arm. The meditations she spent hours a week practising, prepared her for these moments of stillness of being.

Out popped the rabbit. A grey bunny — an adolescent she noted with the experienced squint of her right eye. With just a slight adjustment of her hands she pulled back her right elbow and brought the weapon to face the victim. The rabbit sat back sniffing the air, then with one expelled breathe, lay back, pinned to the ground by the arrow.

That's how quick it was to get caught.

Sofia collected the creature and slung it into her backpack. It was a swift death as she had been taught by Markus her ex-military and off grid friend. She could hear his words in her head as she walked back to her truck.

'You're ready. It's time.'

LET'S GET TO THE NITTY GRITTY

The truth is such a tricky *mind*-field of trickery. What are lies and what is the truth? We are told to trust our leaders and 'the science.' But how do we know if their words are truth and not lies? Tricky truth trickery. Perhaps to comprehend fact from fiction, we should go back to the beginning of this pandemic situation. Darn it, let's go back further. Why don't we just start from 1990.

This was the year that the first S1 spike protein vaccine was issued to a pharmaceutical company. It was also the year that the first canine S1 spike protein coronavirus vaccine was patented. So it seems the Covid-19 vaccine was not entirely rushed through then?

In 1999, Dr. Anthony Fauci wanted to create a virus as a vector for an HIV vaccine. His aim was to take a highly manipulative coronavirus and mutate and chimerically alter it, in order to specifically target the cells inside the human lung. Working with Ralph Berwick from UNC Chapel Hill in the US, they patented coronaviruses to make it more infectious to human beings. Yes you just read that correctly. They turned something that was natural and common place i.e. a cold virus and altered it so it became something toxic and infectious to human beings. They made it worse. Why would they do that?

Still following?

In 2002, Ralph Berwick filed a patent on what they called 'an infectious transmission defective' form of coronavirus. This was one year before SARS 1 in China was discovered. Did you get that? SARS was around a year *after* they created this form of coronavirus.

So let's jump ahead to early February 2020. This is when a veterinarian called Peter Daszak who works with Dr. Fauci and NIAID (National Institute of Allergy and Infectious Diseases), went with the story that a new novel coronavirus came from a bat in a wet market in Wuhan. There are interesting records of an email Daszak wrote, which included the words 'the key driver is the media and economics will follow the hype'. Was he more concerned with investors benefitting from the pandemic than for public health when he wrote, *investors will respond if they see profit at the end of the process?*

Who were the investors you might ask? Interesting Well, none other than Moderna, Pfizer, CDC and Fauci's NIAID.

Interesting right?

Oh and just so you know, in early January 2020, there were gene sequences uploaded from various locations and not just in Wuhan. That's right, this virus was a gene sequence and the first four gene sequences were on December 20, 2019, which predates the first recorded coronavirus patient.

Let's return to Dr. Fauci for a moment. Did you know, that he had been trying to get people to globally uptake his flu vaccine for years? His desire was for one universal vaccine. And did you know that his business has ramped up just under two hundred billion US dollars since 1984? That's a lot of dough huh? Wonder why he is so intent on creating a universal vaccine? Perhaps it could be his obsession with creating a gene therapy future for humankind, where literally, people are a bunch of computer codes managed by a giant pharmaceutical enterprise?

Now it's all getting far-fetched right? I mean it's not like there's any evidence or anything. Oh, there is ...?

Can you imagine if some mad scientist doctor was in cahoots with some major powerful corporate guys to create a toxin gene sequence to put into an injection that was proposed to be put into the arms of everyone in the world? Creating a bio-weapon program to inject the Chinese source computer simulation pathogen into a global population. Oh boy, now that would be bonkers right? Right?

It's not like Moderna, who had never before created a vaccine had anything to gain from being one of the main Covid-19 vaccine suppliers now is it? And that in November 2019, a month before there was ever a pathogen, Fauci was sending spike protein samples from UNC Chapel Hill direct to Moderna. Now how could that be? Surely the virus had not been isolated at that point, so how can samples of it be sent to a pharmaceutical company chosen by Fauci and one that had never before created a vaccine or any injection created for humans? Fauci only announced that Moderna was a front runner for a Covid-19 vaccine in spring 2020, months after the company had received samples of the spike protein that had been patented by the very person sending them the samples. Before the pathogen had even been discovered!

The mind boggles does it not?

And why did the media not run with this information? It was out there for all to see. Why are they sitting on this evidence and doing nothing with it? And why have they never run with any of the stories that would question the authenticity and integrity of statements produced by people like Dr. Fauci? His influence kick started lockdowns, masking and restrictions that negatively impacted people all over the world and have caused millions to have an unknown, experimental drug injected into their arms, based on the fear that people like him have created? Now why would he do that?

Why have the media kept quiet on such key is

sues and why has the global justice system and courts also remained silent when presented with any of these findings and facts? Why indeed!

Perhaps we should be asking more *why* questions rather than saying *okay when?*

Oh, and one more thing. Even if you do not correlate any of this information to a global corrupt system in place that may not have your best interests, let us ask you three more question ...

If these so called vaccines were so beneficial, why is there a blank insert information page in the vaccine box?

What exactly is in these injections and where is the information of possible side effects like in all other medication?

Why is Pfizer allowed not to disclose its data findings on the efficacy and safety of the mRNA vaccines for seventy-five years?

Is there something they don't want us to know?

THE LIGHTBULB

'Hey Jack, do you know how many men it takes to change a lightbulb?'

'Er ... is this a joke Brad?'

'Yup. A really funny one!'

'Okay, so how many men *does* it take to change a lightbulb?'

'One. It takes just one.'

'It's not funny!'

'No, it isn't but look at it this way. Have you ever had a lightbulb moment?'

'Yes of course I have. I think it's called a bright idea.'

'Exactly.'

'So what's your point Brad? I still don't get the joke.'

'Well, if I told you that a very elite group of people had been planning the destruction of mankind for their own purpose, for many, many decades, if not longer, what would you say?'

'I'd say you were mad!'

'Precisely. You'd think I'd lost the plot and probably call me a conspiracy theorist right?'

'Right.'

'So let me tell you a little story. Sitting comfortably?'

'Yeah. Now just get on with the story for Pete's' sake!

'Okay ... There is a long held theory, that a very long time ago, evil beings landed on earth. Some call them aliens, possibly lizards and other said it was fallen angels. You've heard of Lucifer right?'

'Er ... yes of course. But aliens? Come on now Brad. That's a bit far-fetched isn't it?'

'Indeed it is. Incredibly unbelievable. I am not disputing that with you Jack. Just telling the story.

'So go on then, what happened after these lizard aliens, or bad angels fell down from the sky?'

'Mock all you like Jack, mock away. It gets more unbelievable trust me. When Lucifer came to earth, he was pissed with God big time. He wasn't happy with the Big G you see. Wasn't happy that God wanted to create man in his own image. Lucifer was a big cheese angel in Heaven and according to the stories or myths, whichever perspective you have, he was beautiful; the most beautiful of all the higher angels. He was also a narcissist. So when God said he wanted man to be in his own image, he wasn't happy. No sirree.'

'So what happened?'

'God flung him out of Heaven. He was dangerous and had to go.'

'Man, that's harsh.'

'Yes but you have to remember that God is apparently an all seeing God so he must have sensed something was not quite right with this angel Lucifer. Turns out God was right.'

'How come? What did Lucifer do?'

'After being banished from Heaven, Lucifer went to earth. That's where things get juicy. Lucifer hated God and this in turn made him hate man who was made in God's image after all. And so he developed a plan, an evil plan. He was going to turn the very thing that God created with unconditional love and which he created in own image because that's just how much he loved humanity, against God Himself.'

'Jeez. How was he going to do that?'

'See Jack, told you it was a great story ... So Lucifer took a long look at man one day and knew his weaknesses. One sunny day in the land of Eden, Lucifer changed himself into a snake. And the rest of the Creation story we know. Eve ate the apple and the two humans were banished from the Garden of Eden. All because of the snake's deception of man. And therein lies the crux of the story. Man has always been easy to deceive. Of course, throw in a bit of power and a shit load of money and you have the perfect route to revenge.'

'So you are telling me that Lucifer has been hell bent (no pun intended) on seeking revenge against God for creating man in his image against the wishes of Lucifer himself? And because God banished him from Heaven?'

'Yup!'

'Jeez. That's a hard pill to swallow. Seems like such a wild story.'

'Well, it gets uglier and wilder, so hold onto your hat Jack, this ride is about to get bumpy. After Lucifer saw how easy it was to manipulate and deceive man, he didn't stop. Wars, famine, corruption, bigotry, greed, avarice, pride, wrath, lust, gluttony and sloth ... all Lucifer's doing. Man he was having a hell of a time. But still mankind seemed to survive and grow and remain loyal to God despite whatever obstacle Lucifer placed in the way.'

'Yeah, that must have really pissed him off. So what's all this got to do with a lightbulb anyway Brad?'

'I'm getting to that. Patience Jack, patience. So there was Lucifer, throwing all this vile stuff at mankind, but still man did not fall and he still worshipped God. Then he hit onto an idea — what if he got man to destroy himself? That would be the ultimate in revenge right?'

'I guess ...'

'No, really, think about it. God creates man in his image, gives him unconditional love and then lets him get on with it, but always keeping a loving eye on his creation, even sending Guardian Angels and Guides in to give them extra love and protection. It must have been exasperating for Lucifer. Until one day he set his penultimate evil plan in motion.'

'What did he do? Man, as ridiculous as this story is Brad, I admit I'm intrigued.'

'Well, Lucifer, realising that there was a weak element of humanity lurking in the undergrowth of all that was good and moral, formed a connection with a self-proclaimed elite group of men who are influenced by greed and power. This group swore allegiance to Lucifer and not God and thus conjured up a plan to destroy the very thing God loves — mankind itself.'

'Now that is totally unrealistic Brad. Come on! Why on earth would men do that? Surely if they destroyed mankind, then they in turn would be destroyed too?

'Now you're getting into the story Jack. Well done. Why indeed? Great question Jack.

'I'm confused Brad.'

'Hang on in there. So, Lucifer comes up with this idea — offer a group of men all the seven deadly sins and all the riches of the world and all the power of humanity. He had already seen through history, that many men and women would participate in selling their soul for these things if given the chance. Many had hearts more black than darkness itself. Many would turn away from all that was good and all that is God. And this group of men would be given a secret club; the ultimate secret club. To make it attractive, members had to undergo rituals and joining rules to prove loyalty and allegiance to this highly elite group.'

'What kind of rituals Brad?'

'Oh the very worst kind Jack, stuff to make your toes curl and your heart chill to stone.'

'Blimey! And who are these people?'

'They are known by many names but the two you may have heard of are the Cabal and the Illuminati. There are clubs within clubs too; levels of progression, with the penultimate prize being membership to the most elite group. And when a member gets to this level, you can bet your bottom dollar that all sense of decency, morality and all the good stuff that associates man with God, has left the building. They literally have all sold their souls to the devil himself. And these men, for it is mainly men, have no soul or heart. And thus they spare no mercy for those they deem as being 'useless feeders'. That's right, the rest of mankind are waste to them. You getting the picture Jack?'

'So this elite group are what? Controlling the earth under Lucifer?'

'Exactly! Hitler for example, was part of the club. They've been behind some of the worst atrocities in human history. And they have a plan; a brilliant but deadly plan. They are going to euthanize most of the world's population.'

'Waaa...?'

'Yup! They plan to kill the majority of people off. Sounds mad eh?'

'Crazy! How?'

'Glad you asked Jack, glad you asked. Well, since the world's population currently stands at over seven billion, they know that there's no way the planet could continue feeding and sustaining a growing population. So by doing some crazy maths, they came up with a figure of around five hundred million.'

'Five hundred million? That's ridiculous. They'd have to kill six and a half billion people right?'

'Or get them to kill themselves.

'Huh? I don't understand.'

'Think about it Jack. What's the best way to reduce the world's population without them noticing you're doing just that?'

'Man, I don't know!'

'By spinning a tale about a global virus threatening mankind, whisking them up into a frenzy of fear through a highly clever and manipulative psychological operation, combined globally with all the countries in the world saying the same narrative. And then, when the people are so paranoid and hooked into the fear of the virus, they are offered a cure. And this just isn't any old cure. Oh no. It's one that has been researched and devised in various funded laboratories by these elite groups, for decades! It's bloody perfect right?'

'But I thought the vaccine was a good thing?'

'Hah! And that's the thing Jack. That's the clever thing. It isn't actually a vaccine at all. For that would mean it was good for us. It's called that so people wouldn't object to taking it. Do you really think people would take something that had cancer causing chemicals and manufactured spike proteins designed to stick to the cells in your body? Spike proteins that travel around your blood circulation, causing blockages and doing untold damage, as well as totally destroying the very immune system that the Creator gave man to defend itself against viruses in the first place, if they called it was it was? Do you think mankind would willingly and often proudly, agree to be injected with a lethal and unknown concoction of chemicals if they didn't think they were doing good to themselves and their fellow man?'

'No Jack. This is the greatest deception of mankind ever. And watch how the compliant now start to get sick and perhaps even fall. Since they have a compromised immune system, even the common cold is a deadly threat. And they won't add two and two together until the hospitals and morgues are over flowing. Only then will many start asking why and what is in the stuff they took.'

'Blimey Brad? What is it then if it's really not a legitimate vaccine?'

'Sickness and death Brad. Their ultimate control over humanity. Lucifer's ultimate revenge. Destroying the very thing that God loves and doing so by man's own hand. That's right - by man's own hand!'

'Oh wow! So let me get this right Brad Lucifer is the devil or Satan right?

'Yup!'

'And the devil devised a plan to destroy man by using the worse of man to do his dirty work for him? Am I understanding this correctly?'

'Yup. Perfectly correct.'

'But how could we fall for it? I mean, surely we could see through this kinda plan? I mean we are a developed enough species to have some concept of good versus evil right? Darn, I'm so confused. If this were true, then how did we let it happen? '

'Because the majority of people look to leaders to lead them. That's why we elect governments and parliaments and kings and queens and rulers. The majority of people are never going to question the authenticity and truth of the powers. If their elected leaders told them something was true or false, that's what they would believe. Think about it.'

'But we trust these people? And what about the scientists and the doctors and the governing bodies and the CIA and FBI, police, judicial system, media etc. They would see through the plan and stand up against it right?'

'Ah, glad you brought that up Jack. You see, that's where most people are blind and easily led. Coercive words and a clever propaganda of fear tactics played a huge part in the persuasion of people to buy into the narrative. The layers of leadership and authority put in place to guide and lead humanity, are also owned.'

'Owned? By whom. This is getting pretty deep.'

'Well Jack, the reason this plan has been so easy to implement globally, is because most of the countries' governments are in on it. The scientists, judges, heads of police, military, doctors, educators, media and so many more ... they are all part of it. And those that aren't are silenced.

'Silenced?'

'Yeah. One way or another.'

'Wow. It all makes sense now. I saw all those sudden deaths and assassinated presidents, but didn't really think about it. So it's really all connected? But how? How did they do that? Blimey.'

'And that is the lightbulb moment. It only takes one man to change a lightbulb. Welcome into the light Jack. Welcome into the light.

'Wait. Don't leave it at that. I'm scared now. If this is true then we're pretty much all fucked right?

'Nah. Don't panic Jack. You have to remember something really, really important ... the good guys ALWAYS win. Stay good Jack; stay in the light and maybe do a bit more reading up on the guys running the world.

'How do I do that? Hey man, this is all new to me and to be honest, I don't know what to think.

'Yeah, I thought you'd say that. So here's a bit of help to get you started ...

Look up the privately owned companies Blackrock and Vanguard — they own 86% of the world's wealth and almost every company, powerful organisation and institution globally. These are the professed elite of the elite and they care not for you or I and certainly not for the plight of humanity. We are shit on their shoes Jack and utterly expendable. Remember that. Oh and check out the Bilderberg Group too. Really interesting bunch of guys you have there. And maybe the Trilateral Commission whilst you're at it. Some interesting de-population and global control theories that'll make your eyes pop!

Next, look at which companies they own then work your way from there. Who invests in these companies? Now that will shock the hell out of you. Those sweet smiling faces that used to lead the free world? Hah ... not as sweet as you think and nothing is free. Everything is owned Jack and that means they can control and manipulate the world as they see fit.

Ask where the virus originated? Who funds the laboratories and who funds those that fund them? It may shock you to see that most of the world's top philanthropists are also some of the worst examples of humanity ever birthed. The fingers they have in pies, are their own fingers in their own pies. Check out those fingers and pies.

Next research the Covid-19 vaccines. When were the patents put in place for a 'rushed through vaccine'? You'll find that they were filed up to two decades ago in some cases. Strange that eh?

So many things to think about. Who owns and funds the legal system and the medical institutions, the banks, the scientific research programmes, the media, the education system, the military, the police, the FBI, the CIA? Who owns the agencies of the top singers, the bands, the actors, actresses and creative industries? Who owns Hollywood? China has a big stake there and whilst you are looking, check them out too.

Check out the signs — the special handshake of the 'club members', the triangle sign with hands and the triangle with tongue out through the hands over the face. Look out for the one eye covered or closed eye photograph that is popular with celebrities and the hand signal of the Beast. The celebs and the famous and those in power who do these signs. They are the ones who have sold their souls.

Sold to whom you may ask ... well, keep asking and digging and looking. If you want humanity to survive this onslaught, then ask the questions you didn't ask before.

And when you are done asking and you realise the world is darker and more evil than you could ever have imagined, then you look above yourself and towards the Creator, or whomever you call that which is Good and you ask for help to get you through this. And whilst you're doing that, some of us are figuring out a cure to repair the damage these evil monsters helped you to inflict upon yourself and a way to be free of the layered control of the institutions and individuals.

That's the lightbulb moment. If enough people switch on the light, then the whole world will be illuminated and the darkness will dissipate into the undergrowth to hide. Will they ever be destroyed? Who knows and no doubt these evil people will crawl out some day and create some new attempt to destroy or manipulate humanity for their own purposes? But until then, we win this battle and we live another day.'

'Bleeding hell Brad, that's some crazy shit there. If it's true, then that must be the greatest deception of humanity ever. And it's not funny Brad. It's not a funny joke at all.'

'So how many men does it take to change a lightbulb Jack?'

'Dare I say one Brad?'

'Exactly. It just takes one — you! It starts with you. You change that lightbulb, you throw some light on in your darkened corner of the world and watch how others follow suit. It just takes one. It just takes you to spark up the rest of the world to live in the light. Go live in light Jack. Light will always be stronger than the darkness.'

'One more question Brad?'

'Yes Jack ...'

'What happened to those aliens?'

THE LIGHT

If there was any time in your life to solidify your faith, it is now. Whatever that faith looks like, lean into it. Ask whomever you look above to, for help in strengthening your faith. While you're at it, ask for an increase in your trust and for more hope; hope that light will shine where there is darkness. Not just physically, but also in your internal world.

Have hope, have faith and trust that whomever you call Goodness, has your back.

And remember, that light is always stronger than darkness. Flick on the light and chase away the darkness and the shadows. Be the light in your own world and shine out for others so that they too can find their way.

BUILD BACK BETTER

To build back they have to destruct and destroy,
to reconstruct and then re-deploy.
To tear down life as we have always known,
to disconnect our love from the Spirit our soul
calls home.

To build back means something is being
taken.
It is humanity that is being forsaken.
Who wants it better than it was before?
Who wants our normal to be there no more?

They want us gone and want us dead,
could be sweet but hear the truth instead.
Their plan is here but they've not yet won.
We still can fight them, each and every one.

They want a world not for you or me,
just a world for them you see.
Where all the land and all the food,
goes straight to them, for they think that's
good.

Less mouths to feed, the world will last
in hedonism and greed, they'll have a blast.
And the ones of us left alive,
they'll busy us bees in controlled little hives.

A Drop of Truth

Watch the leaders as they say
'Build Back Better, it's a better way.'
For they're all in and we are out,
so it's time they really heard us shout.

Look to God, find your trust,
raise your hope and fight in light, we must.
For light will chase the dark away
and we will live another day,
and perhaps also,
find a more harmonious
and even better way?

THE ONE PERCENT CLUB

Two old men were sitting playing chess outside near the beach. It was a beautifully glorious day in the sunshine and like most every other day, life felt just right. The guy on the left, moved his knight and took away his opponent's last rook.

'Huh!' said the guy on the right distastefully. He wasn't winning and he took the loss of the piece to heart. 'Vanguard you ole bugger, you took my last rook. You did the same last week too.'

'Relax Blackrock pal, you know you always get my bishops,' declared the guy on the left with a smirk.

'Yes but you usually beat me darn it. How do you manage to do it every time?'

'Well,' Vanguard declared in a conspiratorial tone, 'it's all part of the game.'

The guy on the right thought about this for a moment. He had been playing this man for decades and except for a few games here and there, was usually beaten into second place, which greatly irked him, though he had never admitted such to his pal. They had beaten many opponents throughout the years; literally eating up the opposition, to sit at the highly coveted, grand table of this illustrious chess ground.

'You took my bishop!' declared Blackrock fuming.

'Don't sweat it man. You know you'll go for my Queen soon. You always do.' Vanguard chuckled to himself as he placed the black piece next to the others he had gained that day off his opponent.

'Check! Hah!' declared Blackrock in triumph. Oh how he relished making the other man sweat. Justice at last. Perhaps, for the first time in weeks, he might beat him. It was long overdue he declared to himself.

'Checkmate!' announced Vanguard with a declaration of glee.

'What ... no? How?' stammered Blackrock, desperately checking the pieces over and over. 'I don't believe it. How could you get there so quickly?'

'Quickly? We've been playing for decades man!' Vanguard stated in disbelief. 'We've been working our way to the top and squishing all others in the process. You know that no one can touch us; we're the cream of the crop!'

The other man thought about this as he anguished over losing once again and remaining second best to this man he had walked the decades with. Their parents played together and their parents and theirs and so on and so on. They were simply a part of an endearing history of territorial rights and monopolisation. 'I did beat you last month!' he declared skulking.

'Indeed you did and you shall beat me again of that I have no doubt. You are as ruthless and single minded as I am,' declared Vanguard with emphasis and authority. 'We are born to win and be at the top of the mountain. If it isn't me then it is you. It is our destiny!' he declared with the inflated arrogance of a man at the top of the world.

'What happens if we get a challenger to our position?' Blackrock asked with apprehension. 'Or worse, get thrown off the table?'

Vanguard laughed and touched the other fellow's aged hand; a hand that displayed protruding blue veins jumping up out from a milky whiteness. Hands that had never washed a car or laid a flower bed, let alone built a wall or unblocked a toilet. Hands that could never clean off the permanent stain of others' blood, sweat, tears and fears.

'We are the table. We are the challengers. No one is ever going to take away our place. We created this game and we move the pieces where we want to and when we want to, with the one sole purpose of winning. That's what we do. I tend to beat you because I have more desire to be the number one. I am often the victor because I am better and more ruthless than you and you defer to me one way or another. And chess is one way, but there is always another.'

Blackrock remained quiet with his thoughts and instead, surveyed his environment. They were alone except for two more players on a nearby table. Vanguard recognised them as Berkshire Hathaway and Slate Street. Both big players of the game, though Vanguard and Blackrock were hard to beat and hence they usually remained at the top of the tree.

The two men cleared the board and decided to head back to the clubhouse for coffee and a bite to eat. They passed a couple of children playing in the water from a fire hydrant.

'Tsk,' hissed Blackrock in disgust. *Children were only good for one thing* he thought quietly with a sly smirk on his crinkled lips.

'Spare a dime please mate?' a beggar had the gall to ask Vanguard as he passed. The chess champion wrinkled his nose and swallowed back the bile he was ready to spit out at this decrepit excuse for a living mortal. 'Useless feeder,' he whispered as he passed him, ensuring the beggar witnessed the sneering snarl intended just for him.

As they entered the Clubhouse, they both glanced up at the sign and smiled.

THE ONE PERCENT CLUB.

It was etched out in gold ink on a blue background, with the words in bright red, extracted from the blood of three bewildered and terrified young bairns. It stood proudly and in plain sight for all to see. But few took any notice. Well, what was there to take notice of really? Old men playing a game of chess in the outside world and retiring into their secret den to do goodness knows what. What could be wrong with that? After all, it's only a game, right?

LET'S GO TO THE MOVIES

They warned us. The bad guys always tell you their plans. It's the biggest weakness in the film on their behalf and it usually happens just as they think they are about to win. The smell of victory oozes from their pores (cue wicked deranged cacophony of laughter) and as their victim sits confused, fearful or simply biding their time and awaiting their fate, the bad guy/s are spilling the beans.

Then of course, the good guy will somehow get a second wind, a break, a stroke of luck etc., and somehow manages to save the day because he had listened to their oh so evil plan.

So let's take a look at some of those blockbuster movies and TV programs where they already told us what they planned to do, or dropped in clues to indicate their agenda. We'll start the ball rolling and you carry it on. We're sure you can make a bigger list than we have here.

So, grab your popcorn and pull up a seat. We're off to the movies. Oh and a word of warning ... remember, that the big cheeses that run Hollywood are not generally the good guys and many of the studios happened to be owned by the Chinese. Gets better eh?

THE TOMORROW WAR

Latest film to show a virus and the possible destruction of mankind. This one involves aliens. Love an alien film don't you? Anyway, the hero Christ Pratt had to find a cure before humanity either destroyed itself or before the aliens attempted to. At one stage only half a million humans remained before possible extinction. Will Pratt find the cure, kill the aliens and save humanity from annihilation?

AVENGERS ASSEMBLE/ INFINITY WAR/END GAME

Infinity War and End Game are the last in the five Thanos infinity saga films. They are perhaps, the scariest films of all in terms of their correlation with what is happening now, because of Thanos' plan to annihilate fifty percent of the world's population in order to help save the planet from population overload on the planet's resources. In the second film he succeeds in this plan. In the third film, End Game, the good guys win, but boy was it touch and go for a while there. Sorry if that was a spoiler. We suggest you watch it and keep a real open mind! Oh and remember this — Thanos truly believed that what he was doing was a good thing. Not for one moment did he think it wasn't. Though the plot is pretty *en pointe*, this belief that Thanos holds, that killing half the world's population, is actually helping the planet, is perhaps the most chilling part. The global elite believe the same, but for entirely different reasons.

I AM LEGEND

Blimey, this Will Smith film is so scary. A virus turns people into zombies. Real nasty ones too. Smith as the lone human along with his dog, spends his days foraging for food and searching for the cure in his laboratory. This film chills us to the bone. Especially when you consider that on the UK government website there are plans in place regarding dealing with a zombie apocalypse (we kid you not!)

MAZERUNNER FILMS - 1,2,3

Fight for survival of mankind and of individual freedom. More zombies because humans succumb to a zombie causing virus, with the bad guys looking for a cure at the expense of children — that's a bit close to the mark right now but hey, it's just a film right?

INDEPENDENCE DAY

Will Smith again. This time aliens out to destroy humankind. Good ole Smith proving to be the hero again. We love a hero don't we? #goodguyswin

THE MATRIX FILMS

1999 science fiction action film and subsequent Matrix 2 and 3 films, where Neo is awoken into the consciousness of what the world really is. He is 'unplugged' from the simulated reality known as The Matrix. He has to choose a pill — red or blue. Choosing one pill would return him to unknowing what he has been shown and the other pill, would catapult him to see what life is actually like. In this current world of ours, many who call themselves 'awake' feel like they have taken the red bill and unplugged from 'the Matrix'.

THE HUNGER GAMES FILMS

Based in a dystopian world where The Capitol is the city where the ruling elite live a lavish and flamboyant life, whilst those in the District towns of 1-13, live a life of poverty and Capitol control (increasingly so as the Districts move further away from the Capitol. District 13 was destroyed). They are presided over by a man called President Snow. Children from twelve to eighteen years of age from each district are chosen each year to fight to the death in a Hunger Games arena. Purely for the entertainment of those living in The Capitol. Katniss Everdeen volunteers for the Games when her younger sister gets picked. She is spunky and has a natural survival instinct. She soon becomes the rebel the people outside of the Capitol have been waiting for. And so the *mockingjay* movement is born.

President Snow, realising that there is power in numbers and witnessing the increasing popularity of Katniss amongst the people, tells the orchestrator of the Games, Seneca Crane, that,

'Hope: It is the only thing stronger than fear. A little hope is effective; a lot of hope is dangerous.'

(worth remembering!)

SPONGEBOB SQUAREPANTS THE MOVIE

Who would have thought that they would use a Spongebob movie to indicate their plans for global domination? This time it's the tiny, unhappy, greedy Plankton character (he's a plankton btw) who keeps searching for an evil winning plan for purposes of greed, power and domination. It takes his side kick, a female TV style robot, to remind him that the alphabet ends in Z not Y. Hence the evil plan Z is born — customers get a free Chum Bucket hat with their burger. Then Plankton activates the buckets to clamp down onto the unsuspecting customers heads and now they are controlled by Plankton via a remote control. Even the King of Bikini Bottom succumbs.

'All hail Plankton. All hail Plankton.' They are his
slaves and he is all set to 'rule the world!'

Cue Spongebob and Patrick, two adolescent characters who are left with the task of saving the day and Bikini Bottom. How? Self-belief and by blasting the buckets off the trapped heads of the inhabitants of BK when Spongebob loses himself to a moment of being a rock god. No wonder music, singing and dancing has basically been banned across the globe over the past eighteen months. Seems there's hidden power, joy and perhaps the key to freedom, in the vibration of music!

THE TERMINATOR FILMS

AI takes over the world. Man gave them power and that power went to the computer's head and set off a global nuclear attack on mankind. Thank goodness for man's innate desire to survive. Once again, the good guys live to save another day. And you can't knock a bit of Arnie in those films right? But handing power and control over to AI ... humans would never do that now would we?

Oh and as a side, what the heck has happened to the Arnie we once loved. 'Down with freedom!' should be his new mantra. Please can we have the hero Arnie back? Kinda not so keen on this AI robotic, sold his soul version.

CONTAGION and OUTBREAK

Virus/pandemic/fight against time to find a cure films. Too close to the knuckle to be fun viewing. But the good guys eventually win after lots of fear and terror, sickness and death is released onto an unsuspecting world. And of course, there is always the suggestion if not blatant indication, of corruption in power.

V FOR VENDETTA

A must watch. Why? Because that is possibly where we are all heading. Check out China and now Australia. Who would have thought a year ago, that Oz would become a police controlled, segregation state? We are on the brink of a dystopian future and if you can't make the correlation, then you really need to read on. It may be time to start to wake up. Oh and there are many V characters out there. Humanity won't go down without a fight!

THE SIMPSONS

Oh my ... where does the messaging start and where does it end? Creepy!

Okay, we've started the ball rolling. Your turn. Though you may need to make more popcorn!

JUST ONE BOOK OR TWO

Still needing convincing? Well, maybe you should look up two books written by a man called Klaus Schwab - The Fourth Industrial Revolution and The Great Reset.

It's all in there. All of their plans. Step-by-step guides about what is happening, why and where this is all going.

Remember, the bad guys always leave clues or tell you what's happening. It doesn't have to be a film, or a television series. Quite often it's written in black on white as a document format for all to read.

So if you don't already know, you may ask who exactly is this Schwab geezer anyway?

In 1971, at the age of thirty three, Klaus Schwab established what became known as the World Economic Forum. He invited four hundred corporate leaders to attend his meetings in Davos. He later extended invitations to include politicians, media moguls and VIPs from all walks of life. A who's who of the wealthy and elite.

In 1992, he started the Young Global Leaders Program. Who attended these programs you might ask? Well interestingly, some of the current global politicians and corporate leaders who are making the policies and decisions in the world right now, attended Schwab's program. Here are a few you may know — Bill Gates, Angela Merkel, Canadian PM Justin

Trudeau, New Zealand PM Jacinda Arden, President of France Emmanuel Macron to name but a few.

If you note, they are all pushing the narrative in their countries, but the main question, is who is pulling their strings? When you can answer that question, you may be on the right path to your own flight of freedom.

Why have we mentioned Schwab as someone to look into? Well, if you look up the Georgia Stones and read his books and do a little more digging on the global elites and the 'ruling' banking families like Rockerfeller and the Rothschilds and then maybe some of the shareholders of Blackrock and Vanguard, you may get an idea that the world doesn't quite match the fluffy, soft cotton wool cloud the stork brought you in on!

THERE WILL BE A DAY

Soon, there will be a day when it will all make sense. When the veil will fall from your eyes like breathe out of your mouth on a cold wintery day. Soon. It won't be too far away. Not too long to wait.

Do you remember what life was like before? Before this madness knocked and rapped upon your door? Where were you in life and what were your thoughts? Were you fulfilled or unhappy of sorts? Did you love your job? Was it nine to five? Did the office job banter make your spirit dead or alive? That Friday feeling, did it last the week, or did your weekend already feel bleak?

Regardless, so much has gone and may never come back. Do you feel abundance or wallowing in lack? That holiday, trip to see your mates, dinner at Granny's, before she sadly met her fate. Jump on a ferry, or hop on a plane, will we do all these things once, or ever again?

How did it happen, how did we lose? This freedom of ours; did we all snooze? When we weren't looking, did the thief come at night, to bind all our hands and blind all our sight? To whisper sweet lies into our cute little ears and replace all our reasoning, with a shit load of fears.

Some watched as they hacked away at our brains, sweet nothings and promises with little to gain. But alas those untruths and trusting their words, will soon seem outrageous and really absurd.

A day will come soon, there is little to doubt, when those that are jabbed, will scream and will shout. For the veil when it falls and reality sets in, will be devastating for all who blindly fell in. Into their lies that they conjured for you, so that you would succumb, first to one dose, then two, then three and then four; what will you say when they ask for much more?

But please do not fear, for fear feeds their game and they've set this all up in the Darkest of names. Take heart, have hope and live well in trust, the key to survival is faith, it's a must.

Praise your Creator, the One full of Love, look not to the TV instead look above. The war isn't over, the victory not set. There is hope for us all from the One we know and have met.

THE STORM

It's coming from the East
The East you say?
How could you know?
Are you a God or soothsayer, hey?

From the East I say,
Soon, some soon day,
In a robe of sun
And young,
The storm, it will come.

And he will say he is for,
But he's really against
And anti the light,
For darkness his mist.

There is a storm, it's on the way.
Beware the storm,
That comes soon,
One soon awful day.

THE LOST WHO DO NOT SEE

They cannot see the light
no matter how we fight.
Their eyes they stay closed,
their minds shut tight.

They will not, cannot see the light;
the Lost.
The ones who do believe
untruths,
and thus are just not free.

Like sheep they live in pens
because they need to follow,
The Piper and his piper men,
so the bitter pill they swallow.

Alas the sheep are lost
but there's a real shepherd in their
midst.
One who will not give up on them,
no matter how much they will resist.

He knows that they must live,
despite their penned in state
and no matter how hard the odds,
humanity will survive,
the evil's wicked fate.

THE SPOKEN WORD

Trust not the spoken word,
from box or news stand land.
The stuff that spouts forth
from the ones who sold their hand.
Trust not the lies they tell
sludge from mouths and a black heart soul,
that fell to hell a long, long time ago.
Trust not their spoken words
and lies of myths and so absurd.
Don't, just don't,
believe one government
or media spoken word.

ONE DAY I WANT TO BE A JOURNALIST

Dear Diary,

One day when I grow up, I want to be a journalist. I love to write and I have a really inquisitive mind. I will join one of the big newspapers or maybe even one of those news channels on telly. I might even be an anchor one day!

But want I really want to do is tell peoples' stories. I want to give people a voice and let the world read about them. I'm going to be one of those journalists who tells the world the truth about what's going on and about what happens in peoples' lives. I want to be a voice of the people.

When I grow up Diary, I am going to become an investigative journalist. I can't wait!

Billy. Aged thirteen and a half.

'Billy, we need you to run the story on how the vaccine is helping children to go visit their grandparents.'

'But boss, I've been working on a great story about the cover up of that internet CEO's death the other day. Man, this story is going to blow big time. You know, it wasn't suicide: he was killed. And it's who was involved in his death and why, that's the big news. I got all the evidence. Shit, this is a BIG story! It's the chance I've been waiting for forever. It's huge!'

'Forget that story Billy, we need you to write about kids looking forward to seeing their grandma now the vaccine rollout is in full speed. We are push-ing the vaccine and encouraging the people to get it.'

'But this story ... I've been working hard on it for the past coupla' weeks. I'm telling you Dan, it's head-line stuff. There are some big names involved. Heads are gonna roll over this when it comes out. It's a real scoop I'm telling ya!'

'You won't be running the story Billy.'

Billy stares at his boss in disbelief.

'I don't understand.'

Dan puts his arm around Billy's shoulder and moves him towards the wall and out of earshot of everyone else. 'We *can't* run that story Billy.' He simply stares into his face and hopes the penny drops.

It doesn't. Billy still doesn't get it.

'Why? It's a great story; a front page headline story.'

Dan sighs and just above a whisper says,

'*They* won't let you run it. Get it?'

Billy felt tears of rage and disbelief crawl up from his chest to his tear ducts, but men don't cry so he willed them back down, but not before Dan saw the emotion in the younger man's face. He too felt sad, but he also wasn't losing his job anytime soon. He had an ex-wife, two kids and a girlfriend with a child on the way to pay for. Plus a mistress, well, his girl-friend wasn't into sex due to the throwing-up and his sex drive was through the roof right now. Women and homes were darn expensive!

Plus he was getting paid extra to push the vaccine out and he wasn't going to let some breaking news story ruin that. That was old school journalism. And though the hack part of him yearned for the thrill of that type of new scoop exposure, he had to think of paying the bills and of that huge bonus promised at the end of Fall. Besides, his bosses would never run the story.

'But it's such a great story Dan. The guy was set-up; murdered for speaking out. The people need to know the truth. Isn't that part of our job, to tell the news, to tell the truth? To expose government lies and corporate corruption? Isn't that our job?' Billy could hear his voice was a little high pitched and wild since he was holding back the emotion, but he didn't care. He had worked so hard to get to this point in his career. This was a pivotal turning point in his journey; this story was his big break. This scoop was going to make him.

'Billy, we have no choice. The big bosses, the ones who own the news corp and the ones who own them ... they are not going to let us run it. I'm sorry. Geez, I really am.'

The two men looked at each other. Both minds alight on different trains of thought. Both considering their paid employment. But one was thinking of the vacation in Palm Springs his bonus would grant him and the other was thinking of paying his rent and feeding himself and his young wife and two-year-old child.

'Why Dan? Why won't they run it? They could still run the other stories about vaccines. I mean it's not like we don't run them *every day*? In fact, that's all that's in the news these days. The people must be getting tired of it? They'd love a story like this. It would be a huge distraction if nothing else.' Billy felt his words would appeal to the journalist mind of his boss.

Again Dan sighed and drank in the animated face of his younger colleague. He had to admit to admiring his tenacity. Pre-pandemic, he would have been on his side and agreed wholeheartedly. Billy would have got his headline and they would have sold shit loads of papers that week and run it on stations, did follow up interviews and pieces etc. Billy's name as an investigative journalist would have been set. Darn it, he'd probably even get a book deal out of it.

He got it, he really did. But his own job meant more than the rise of another's career. Besides, if he run it, they would both lose their jobs and he wasn't certain if they could be guaranteed to keep their lives either. Too many people were suddenly disappearing these days, or they were suspiciously committing suicide, or suddenly dying of a heart attack despite no previous heart issues. He knew what was out there. He was once a top journalist himself and he would have got all hot and bothered under the collar too if he had a story like this and couldn't run it. Billy wasn't that dissimilar to himself. Except he hadn't yet sold out. But needs must.

'Billy, I like you, I really do, but here's the rub. We can't run the story. End of. The bosses won't let you. You're right about it being a distraction and that's the thing: the last thing they want is a distraction from Covid and the vaccine. Think about it,' he whispered to his ear, 'ask yourself why?'

Billy looked at the face of his boss. What was that? A flash of fear? He watched as droplets of sweat accumulated on Dan's forehead and then escape and land on the older man's shirt collar. It wasn't hot in the building, in fact, it was always cool if anything. No, this was anxious sweat.

'They WON'T let this story come out. Got it?' Dan said through the grit of his teeth.

'Yeah. I got it.' Billy relented with a sigh.

Dan visibly shrunk with relief. He didn't have to dismiss a darn good employee after all. 'Good. Now do me a favour, bin that story and run with the kids and grandma one OKAY?'

'Yeah, okay.'

Dan stood there watching him, waiting and Billy looked at the story in his hand with remorse. His heart was heavy as he threw the bundle of papers in the bin. He would delete it from his computer later. He thought about his wife Charlotte and their sweet little girl and how they relied on him to work and provide for him. Despite his journalist heart, his love for them was greater.

'Good man,' Dan said as he patted him on the arm and left.

Billy walked towards his desk, but he knew he left a large part of him behind. He was no longer an investigative journalist but a reporter. He reported on what he was told to report. He knew this as he grabbed a coffee from the machine before he slumped into his chair. He sighed and knew that he had, in the space of twenty minutes, become another media puppet. That was the day that Billy Garcia was to develop a drinking habit that would never go away and see his family leave him in exactly four years from that day.

Meanwhile Dan returned to his office and took one pill for his heart and another for his anxiety. Before the meetings with his bosses last year on the way his paper was to be run and the stories they could and could not report. Dan was in perfect health save a tendency to eat too many donuts, which he blamed on his police man dad, who brought home donuts for him and his brother every Friday night. That was, until his pop got a gunshot wound during a robbery shoot out, which left the old man with a permanent limp and an addiction to daytime TV. He sighed as he sat back in his chair and wondered how the hell he had managed to become the person he had. He felt for Billy, he really did, but he knew his bosses' were not the type of people to mess with. He was simply surviving and as sad as that was, it was working for him right now, so why rock that boat?

At his desk, feeling hypothetically disembowelled and lobotomised, Billy vacuously started to type-up the story on kids, grandparents and the wonders of an experimental drug called an mRNA vaccine. Though he didn't use the word 'experimental'. He thought better of it.

Meanwhile, Eddie the post boy was passing the bin where Billy had thrown the discarded story. Eddie was twenty-three, so a few years younger than Billy and never had a break in his life. His step father was an alcoholic and his mother lost her mind many years ago. His brother was in jail and his sister married someone just like their father and their step father who came after him. Eddie wasn't a bad guy and wanted to be a journalist in his younger life. When he was thirteen, his school had a visit from a top national journalist, who, as a child, attended his school. He was in awe of this guy and the stories he told. He made journalism sound awesome. So when he went home that evening, he wrote this in his diary: for he also, like the young Billy, kept a diary.

Dear Diary,

One day I am going to be a great journalist. I am going to travel the world and be a famous writer.

He didn't write much more in his diary after that, since his step father beat up on him, his mum and his siblings regularly. Alas, his dreams also got beat up out of him. His life wasn't so sweet in his mid to latter teens and he ended up in trouble at school and in dead end jobs. He got the job as a post boy on the paper because he happened to make a comment to a guy in a bar about wanting to have been a journalist when he was younger. This guy knew another guy who knew a guy looking for someone to replace someone in a post boy job.

So it was a complete coincidence that morning, that Eddie happened to be walking past at the exact moment that he overheard Dan tell Billy to drop the scoop of the century story and run one about vaccines. Eddie was sick of hearing about the pandemic, Covid and the bloody vaccines. He heard they weren't even real vaccines but some toxic shit that will probably end up killing you more than the virus would.

So, it was with those thoughts and the thoughts of feeling like a failure and a drop out in society, that sought him to put his hand into that bin and retrieve the discarded story. He folded it and stuffed it up his jumper until he got a chance to put it somewhere safe until home time.

He had a feeling that this was big. He was too fearful to look at it in the building in case someone caught him. He was respectful after all and really loved the job despite the poor pay and slow career prospects. Being there however, re-ignited a dying ember of hope in him; a lost memory of some place he was meant to be and something he was destined to be doing.

After work, when he got back to his scruffy, one room apartment, on the not so pretty side of town, he grabbed a beer from the refrigerator and dared to read the story. Halfway through, he got up, knelt on the floor and offered up thanks to God. Life he felt, was about to change dramatically for Eddie Brown.

CRONYISM

He gave it to his mate
who was a buddy in his club
or maybe it was someone
who owned a local pub?

Because they swore allegiance
to the ones who own the world
they gave them all the contracts
and no-one questioned it at all.

The guy that got the job
the woman sucking dick
there seems to be a lot of it
this mutual back rubbing kinda trick.

That's how to run a country
That's how to win a war
and if you don't agree
then you're out of someone's door!

FLY ON THE WALL

There once was a fly minding its own business sniffing around a dumpster outside a building in a city someplace somewhere. It noticed a window open and in its short life experience, open windows in buildings usually led to food or shit and at that moment, either would suffice, since the dumpster wasn't producing anything of lick-able value. Once inside the building, the fly followed its nose and hunted down a smell. There was definitely something worth exploring in another room further down the hall and into another part of the building.

Since the fly liked to stop and explore every surface, his food hunt was taking quite some time. He was busy licking some crusted old food from the underside of a large wooden table in one empty room, when it suddenly started to fill up with people. The fly, in his short life span, knew people and flies weren't exactly best friends, so he quickly darted to hide atop a curtain pole, where he would sit unnoticed until he got the chance to make a break for freedom. However, once the people were in, the door was locked shut and there were no windows to escape out of. He really hoped he would get home in time for supper with the missus and the kids. *Bless them* he thought. It was only a week ago that they were little maggots crawling out of a dumpster. How quickly they had grown!

With nothing better to do, he watched the men and remarked to himself how strange they looked in their aprons and robes. He noticed that they were mainly white and old, though a handful of the men were younger. But they were all so serious and grey and self-contained. They didn't smell like the people outside either. He couldn't help himself, he was intrigued. The men milled around in a circle doing some reciting of words. It was all very serious. Then they sat down to talk.

There was a knock at the door and someone entered in with a bunch of drinks and pastries and since the fly knew that pastries meant food on floor, he decided to hang out a bit longer. So he busied himself cleaning his face whilst the men chatted. He could wait.

But a word caught his ear and piqued his interest. The word he heard was 'Plan'. He loved a good gossip to his spouse after a day of buzzing around scouring for food. So he decided to move a little closer and listen more attentively.

'It's all going to Plan?' one of the men said to the others.

'Yes indeed. It has been so easy. Much easier than I thought it would. Hardly any resistance across the world,' said another.

'The sheep have been conditioned to believe whatever they have been told. It's truly beautiful to watch,' said the first man to speak. The fly noted that the other men revered him more than the others, so he guessed he was the hierarchy of the group.

'Have there been any complications that we should concern ourselves with?' the leader man asked.

Another of the group spoke up.

'Not really. The injection is doing exactly what we predicted — slow adverse reactions and just a few thousand reported deaths, but we hide or falsify the true data. Thus it's generally unnoticed by the people and of course, by throwing in the variants idea, they are convinced that the injection is protecting them and that it's the non-compliant creating a new wave by spreading the new variant. Of course there isn't a variant, simply their immune systems not responding to any type of virus and of course, the spike proteins attacking them internally. It's perfect and entirely to Plan. They may clock on eventually, but they haven't figured it out yet.'

'Excellent. Exactly as we anticipated,' the leader man said. 'What has the take up been like globally?' He directed this at a wiry man with glasses and a long nose who sat to his left.

'We had some dissenting countries, but we dealt with them before they became an issue. Every country is now on board,' said the wiry man.

'Great news. And of those countries giving trouble, what did you do?'

'We replaced the leaders with more agreeable ones.' The wiry man smirked as he said this. The fly shivered as he watched the men's faces. He had never before seen such cold and un-human like people in his short, but experienced life.

'Excellent news!' declared the leader man.

'How long before we have one hundred percent injection uptake?' the leader man looked directly at the wiry man with this question.

'Oh they will all succumb; one way or another.' the wiry man answered with his grimacing smile. The fly actually felt something like fear watching this man speak. The man was like no man he had ever seen before. His blood even smelled different.

'For the Plan to succeed, we will need all humans to be injected, from babies to old. I don't care if we have to bolt them to the ground to do it: they all need this toxin. It's key to the next phase of the Plan. Do you understand?' The leader man almost shouted the last three words. And the other men grunted in reply.

'Nothing will stop the Plan,' declared the wiry man with his sly, cold smirk.

'When Fall comes, they will start to fill up the hospitals and their morgues. As the cold viruses and flu season attacks, their immune systems will not be able to fight; the injection would have seen to that. This is a time when questions might be asked and the sheep rebel and fight back. It is imperative we do not allow that to happen do you hear? Nothing can get in the way of the Plan. Nothing and no one!' the leader declared. He got up and started walking around the room. The fly, feeling conspicuous despite his minutiae size, cowered. There was something about these men that filled him with blood chilling fear.

'For centuries, our forefathers have ruled this world with intricate and subtle conditioning of the people. From childhood vaccines to education, religious indoctrination, to medical treatments and social ideologies. We have been at the forefront of all of this and have created a layered system of control and power, intricately assembled so that one day, this day, we could take over the world completely and rule it as we have chosen to see fit. One World Government with the people totally under our control. Men, if they fart we will know!' The men chuckled at this.

'We all know that earth cannot sustain a growing population and that these useless, bottom feeders are sucking the planet of all natural resources. If left alone, the planet would crumble to dust. So we are merely helping it to survive by starting again. We do not need all these people. We only require a handful to sustain the land and produce what is required for our needs. Man needs to survive gentlemen, but not mankind as we now know it. Extermination of eighty-five percent of the human race, along with their ridiculous pets and animals, is the only way Earth can survive as a sustainable planet. It is the only way *we* can survive. This is the Plan and we must not lose sight of it. Remember — Build Back Better. Nothing can stand in our way!'

'Hear, hear!' the other men grumbled after the leader man's speech.

Wow thought the fly. *And I thought I was meant to be the pest. Seems everyone in the outside world is as much of an unwanted pest as me.* But the fly didn't feel happy with this knowledge. Instead, he felt desperately sad for humanity, which was quite absurd since he knew man would swot him dead at any given opportunity.

He was just about to fly closer to the door to make a hasty exit if the opportunity arose, when he heard the wiry man pipe up. His words chilled him to core of his tiny being.

'Why don't we just kill everyone now and reclaim the planet?' he asked.

All the men looked at him and then to the leader, who drew a long, knowing smile across his face.

'Most will die but we need some alive to enslave. Women and babies particularly, for our own needs,' he smirked. The others smirked and nodded back. We need the blood of the young to slow down the ageing process and we have to ensure we have sacrificial humans for our rituals. We can't get rid of everyone. That would be too easy and not in *our* best interests.'

One of the other men who hadn't yet spoke, piped up. 'We also need some of them to become humanoids. These will be our slaves.'

'Yes indeed.' said the leader nodding in affirmation at the man who spoke. 'We will need many slaves.'

'I have a question.'

126

The men all looked to a short, plumper, younger man who had not yet spoken.

'What about all those who are currently complicit with the Plan? The country's leaders, their minions, the complying media, some of the scientists and doctors, the institutions and Associations, the Church and religious leaders? Those in Hollywood and the music industry? What happens to those? Surely we can't take everyone with us on the next part of the Plan?'

'Good question,' said the leader acknowledging this man. He took a sip of his coffee and sat upright before speaking.

'Some will be exterminated and some will remain. It will depend on their sworn allegiances, where they stand in the organisation and whether or not they are in it for the greater good or for their own desires. Gentleman ...' the leader man addressed the group, looking at each man individually, 'there is something important we must remember about man. He is weak. He is driven by ego and insecurities, which is why he has been so easy to manipulate and control for so long. We have learned that through the use of linguistic and psychological programming, we can convince them that black is white and so on. They have been absorbing this conditioning for decades and the invention of the media platforms, has made this conditioning so much easier for us in our desire to control and contain them. Free and independent thought is our enemy. They must not be allowed to have this knowledge and run free with it. Even those that are signed up to the Plan must be watched. ANY dissention will be stopped. Do we agree on that?' The men all nodded or mumbled

'Agreed.'

The leader smiled and nodded his head then got up and walked around the room touching the right shoulder of each seated man. Then continued.

'We must learn the lessons from the failed Nazi regime. We had them in the palm of our hand at one point. The Plan was set in place and being carried out to almost perfection ... Hitler, one of our esteemed brethren, did an immense job to create a cancel culture of one type of peoples. With the weight of our support, the Nazi regime almost achieved what we are achieving now. One century later, we are in World War Three: the final war. This time we shall not be defeated. We have learned through the mistakes of the Nazi regime. This time we have globalized our propaganda, psychological programming and social conditioning. We have not retained it to one country or to a few types of peoples. We do not see Nazi Germany a failure, but a lesson. It proved how easy it was to control people through propaganda. We have since learned what we have to do to control the entire world. And congratulate yourselves men, it was a lot easier than we originally thought it would be. The end is indeed in sight.'

The men all patted each other and laughed and smiled with self-congratulation. And it was in that moment, despite all he had just heard about world domination and a Plan to annihilate mankind, the fly noticed something very important (but he was a fly so he didn't realise quite how important). He noticed how easy it was for the leader to get the men to do as he asked. He told them to congratulate each other and that's exactly what they did without questioning.

Man is so easy to manipulate. Even the manipulators can be manipulated. And whilst the men were grumbling and laughing and distracted by their instruction to pat each other for their efforts, the leader briefly left the room. The fly took this opportunity to dart out the door. He had heard enough. Just before he headed for the exit out of the building, the fly noticed the leader man walking into another room. He glanced in before the door shut and saw him shake hands with two beings. The fly gasped in his fly gasping voice. He had never seen a creature like that before.

So glad I came back as a fly. The fly thought as he zoomed out the building never to re-enter those walls again. *At least I am free.*

And as the fly, distracted in his thoughts by what he had just seen and heard, drew closer to his home under the lid of a dumpster bin, he did not see the bird perched on a nearby house, swoop down for her lunch. She loved nothing better than juicy, fat, knowledgeable flies.

THERE WAS A PLAN

When did it start, this Plan?
Was it before the time of my great great
grandfather's gran?
Or way before then
when the world was bare
when Jesus wasn't even there?

Did it evolve with greed
or knowledgeable despair
or did another species put it there?
Oh boy, if so,
that's so darn unfair!

WE'VE BEEN HERE BEFORE

Remember that yellow star, the burning of books, the train rides to nowhere, the funny goose walk, the experiments, the lampshades and products made from human hair and skin, the pits of broken bodies, the walking skeletons, the annihilation, the pile of shoes, the museum, the stolen properties and possessions; the starvation, the beatings, the discrimination, the segregation, the second class citizenship, the exclusion from shops, bars, restaurants, events, nightclubs, the 'them and us' mindset?

It started back then as it's started here, right now, in this decade, this year, with them, with us, with you. *Divide and conquer* they say. But who is being divided from whom and who really are being conquered? Who are the victors? You? Is it really all for you? Is your life worth the extinction of these others? And then there is no guarantee that they won't come after you.

They said it would never happen again. We believed them. We had The Trial; we set rules and put boundaries in place. We swore on the memory of the lost millions ... THAT IT WOULD NEVER HAPPEN AGAIN. Are you okay with that?

Haven't we been here before?

A MAN CALLED IVOR

There was a man called Ivor
Mectin, his surname,
he wanted to be famous,
but no one knew his game.

He tried his best to change that,
to fit into the crowd,
but a big ole burly bouncer said,
'Oi, get out, you're not allowed!'

Poor ole Mr. Mectin,
he tried his best he did,
and if they could only let him in,
it would only cost a few small quid.

For he had a real fun friend,
a medic none the less,
HQQ they called him
a shorter name they found was best

Now HQQ and Ivor could help those who
failed the test,
but alas these worthy friends
were never sought as best —
to help out those who failed the test.

It seems the in-crowd were not in favour,
of old trusties just like them.
They didn't make much money,
so didn't fit into their Plan.

But Ivor and his mate,
are good ole kind of boys,
and so are waiting in the background,
for you to make some noise.

#MOCKINGJAY: Part 3 Back Pack

Sofia took her bow and arrow into the forest. Night time was calling away the sun, who, reluctant to leave the young woman alone, meandered above the hills long enough for her to exit her truck and check her back pack. Then it bid her well and allowed the moon to step in and take its place. The moon, did his best to assist her mission by shining as brightly as he could. The clouds were kind also and for once, did not obstruct the light of the ancient, slivery moon.

The young woman, already fearful internally, was grateful of the moon's offerings. Darkness was not a friend, so the light was truly welcome.

The day before, Markus had called her.

'It's time,' was all he said. Last night, for the first in a long time, she opened a bottle of wine and stayed up until the early hours reading about warrior mentality and scouring her vast collection of books for whispers of wisdom and glimmers of hope. At least Archie finally got some sofa stoke time.

She didn't go out the following morning. Instead, she ate, rested, slept and meditated. Nothing she did however, could prevent the anxiety eating away at her insides. *Trust* and *faith*, were words delivered to her consciousness when she begged for help to get her through the long day. Never before had she both longed for and dreaded the passing of time to become one awaited moment: the moment she found 'herself in right now.

She felt extreme fatigue as she slung her back pack over her right shoulder and the bow and arrow on her left. She wore black, her face masked black, camouflaged in paint as Markus had showed her via a zoom meeting the week before. They were in different states and because of his associations, knowledge and connections, Markus was forced underground and off grid. She reflected in that moment, that her life felt like the film Eraser, but there was no Schwarzenegger character to assist her with the bad guys. She was on her own for this one.

'This is it Sofia,' she murmured to herself as she adjusted her pack onto her back. 'It's do or die time.'

JUST ...

Just a few weeks to flatten the curve
Just a few feet
Just a mask
Just protecting granny
Just protecting the NHS
Just a school
Just a business
Just a jab
Just another jab
Just a tremor
Just a blood clot
Just a heart attack
Just one death
Just one kid
Just one baby
Just a flight
Just a holiday
Just a nightclub
Just an event
Just a shop
Just a school
Just another mask
Just another jab
Just a cough
Just a hospital
Just another death

Just another death
Just another jab
Just another booster
Just a prison camp
Just a forced injection
Just to silence the unwashed
Just to protect you
Just to protect the NHS
Just to protect them
Just to protect us
Just annihilation
Just cause
Just our Plan

A CHAT IN THE PARK WITH GRANDPAPPY

'New World Order? What's that'? Jake asked his grandpappy as he sat with his grandfather on a bench in the park. It was a warm summer day in June and they sat beside a lake watching young moms feed the birds and the ducks. It was Jake's turn to spend an hour with the old boy today and though he resisted because he had a basketball jam with the guys planned for midday, something inside told him to spend as much time with the old guy as he could.

'How old are you?' asked the old man.

'Fifteen Paps.' Jake rolled his eyes. Paps never remembered their ages.

'Whipper snapper!' the old guy remarked. 'You should know more stuff then!' he said as he nudged the boy's right arm and snorted.

Jake rolled his eyes again and nudged him back.

'So go on, what's all this stuff you are talking about?'

The old guy looked slyly at his grandson.

'Did you get the things I told you to get?'

'What? The extra supplies for mom, the batteries, outdoor fire stuff etc? Yeah I got them. I asked dad for the money for new trainers like you suggested, so I didn't have to ask Mom.' The boy nodded to himself wistfully.

'Good boy!' said the old man patting him on his knee. Jake smiled inwardly. It was this tactility, this gentleness in the old man that he loved the most.

'The New World Order son is something you need to look up.' the old guy started looking ahead to a far off place in his mind, 'you'll need to know what's coming and you need to know why it's coming and who you're dealing with.'

'Paps, what does that mean? You do know I'm just a kid right and this conspiracy theory stuff you keep throwing me is way over my head!'

'Was I wrong two years ago when I told you there was going to be a pandemic caused by a virus?'

'No, but ...'

'Was I wrong in December 2019, when I said that was our last Christmas as a free people?'

'No, but ...'

'Was I wrong when I told you they were going to close stores and businesses, stop you going to school and keep everyone locked up at home?'

'No Paps, you weren't, but ...'

'Was I wrong when I told you that they would start to take away every freedom you had without you even noticing and even that you would be asking them to?'

'Did you say that?' asked Jake incredulously and with a dubious look.

'Yes boy I did. Didn't I tell you that they would be making people take a vaccine to stop the spread of this virus and that if you didn't take it you would be punished?'

'Yes Paps and I didn't believe you.'

'I know,' said the old man with a serious, but admonishing look on his face. 'And didn't I tell you something else?'

'Paps you told me so many things since dad left, that I can't remember half of what you told me! You have to admit, that some of what you said, like aliens and an underground group of evil men in cahoots together to destroy mankind, is pretty bat shit crazy, right?'

The old man turned to the boy, who at first refused to meet his stare. Slowly Jake turned his head towards his grandfather. 'What?' was all he could think of to say.

'So if I was right about all the other things and all those have now transpired, what makes you think I'm wrong about this boy?'

Jake had offended the old guy. He hated to do that. His grandfather was ex-military; really high up too from what his dad told him. Maybe even as high as they could go. He knew a lot about a lot and he was never wrong. Even on the first day at high school when his grandfather dropped him off since both his parents were working. He had been retired over fifteen-years by then and was always around for Jake.

'See that boy over there? The short one in the blue sweater, with the navy backpack?' asked the old boy to his then nervous grandson.

'Yeah I see him,' recounted Jake.

'Stay away from him. He's the class bully.'

Jake never told his grandfather how right he was. It took him three months of constantly being harassed by that boy before he found the guts to punch him square on the jaw one day, just as his paps had taught him. That was the day he gained respect from his classmates and learned that his grandfather had some kind of sixth sense.

So Jake decided to sit and listen to this wise old man, as he spewed out an incredulous tale about a global elite group of men, who through decades, if not centuries, had created a layered domination structure over the world, which incorporated banking institutions, media, pharmaceutical companies, academies, research laboratories, universities, hospitals, science, big tech giants, so many other business and authorities and associations and most surprisingly off all to Jake, since that was where his future career interests lay, almost every political environment possible. They basically ruled the world Jake was hearing.

'How is that possible? How have they been allowed to do that?' asked the boy shaking his head in disbelief.

'Jake, man has always had good and bad in his soul. We were born with free will. You can be influenced by good thoughts in your life, or by bad ones. Of course, who is to define what is good and what is bad? But that is another subject altogether,' added the old man with a wink. He looked ahead and sighed. His eyes bypassed the shimmering lake and the kids playing ball and the young moms sharing a picnic and gossiping loudly. Instead, his sight was focused on a place beyond that, within his thoughts.

'Mankind is in real danger Jake. These guys, with their New World Order, well ... Well, they think they are winning. And that's both bad and good for the rest of us.'

Jake looked at his grandfather, whom in that moment, looking sad and vulnerable, he loved more than anything in the world.

'Paps,' the young boy said as he placed his smooth teenage hand over the old man's crinkly, veiny one. 'It's going to be alright.'

'Perhaps,' was all the guy said without a smile or words of hope. 'Perhaps. But it depends ...'

'Depends on what Paps?'

'On whether people can step out of the game they are in and see that they are being played.'

The two men were silent for a moment, as both were lost in the scenario of their thoughts. Then the young man had an idea.

'You said it was good and bad for us Paps. What do you mean by that? Why can it be good if all this bad stuff is true and they really are trying to control, manipulate and kill us off?'

The old man raised a slow smile. Finally, the boy understood; finally he was thinking; finally he was stepping out of the game.

'Because they already told us what they are going to do,' the old guy said with a wink.

TESTING, TESTING ONE, TWO THREE

'He said it himself didn't he — it shouldn't have been used for detecting a virus in the body. That guy who invented it, the one with the woman's name. He said it wasn't set up for that. And then strangely enough, he was dead. Deaded, just like that. Another heart attack or suicide, or did he simply die in his sleep? *Pneumonia* you say? Blimey, how ironic. What's that you say he said?'

They should only run the test at a 24 cycle-threshold of amplifications and under to be accurate in order to depict an accurate reading of the virus present.

'Well that sounds clear enough. What? They don't? Well what do they run the cycle at then?'

37 to 45 cycle-threshold?

'Really? Well what does that mean?'

Running at 35 cycles produces 97% false amplifications. So, at 45 cycles the test is so sensitive that it picks up every miniscule molecule of virus, live or dead, and thus it isn't at all accurate and that's why there are so many false positives. And the cycles can be manipulated to produce the results they want? For example, before the vaccine rollout, they were run at 37-45 cycle amplifications and just after the rollout, they run them at around 28 cycles to depict they were working.

'Blimey! Well how is that allowed then? What does that mean, *'exactly'?* Are you being sarcastic? Mmm. This is serious stuff you know. Peoples' lives and livelihoods depend on accurate testing. I know you *know*, but I'm just saying that's all. I'm sure the scientists know what they're doing, 'trust the science' and all that!'

We are only allowed to listen to some of the science?

'I thought science was science right? The who?'

The Great Barrington Declaration?

'What's that when it's at home? Sounds like a treaty from the olden days. 'The Great Barrington Declaration!' I'm not mocking. Okay, maybe I was a little, but what is it anyway?'

A group of scientists, doctors and lawyers and others, questioning the narrative and offering a different perspective.

'Perspective on what?'

On the narrative.

'What the heck is that?'

The line the governments, the WHO, the FDA, CDC and the media are giving us.

'Well why wouldn't they tell us the truth? Are you suggesting these people aren't telling us the truth? Why would they lie to us? Why would they tell us one thing if it was something else?

Exactly

'Exactly? So are you saying that there's another perspective on this whole pandemic thing and that there's thousands and thousands of doctors and scientists saying something different to the 'narrative' we are being given? Really?'

There are treatments other than the vaccine for Covid and to prevent Long Covid but we are being kept away from them.

'Well why would they do that? Surely they have our best interests at heart? Why are you laughing? So going back to the PCR test, explain the cycles meaning. I don't really understand.'

A test should be run at 24 cycle amplifications and under, so that the test would be more or less accurate. But over 24 and especially at a 45 cycle-threshold, the test is potentially inaccurate because it can pick up traces of someone else's old virus or old virus particles in the air or in the body if the person once had Covid, but no longer does.

'Okay, so my question is, that if you know this and aren't a scientist or a doctor, why don't the doctors and scientists know this too? It would save a lot of hassle and heartache for everyone right? I mean didn't they base the whole 'public health threat' on these tests? Weren't we in lockdowns and wearing masks and not touching each other and saying everyone was asymptomatic BECAUSE of the results of these tests?'

They do know.

'What do you mean *'they do know*?' I don't understand. They can't all be lying.

Some of them are in on it and the others are just doing their jobs and not asking questions.

'Okay that explains a lot. But hey, that's still unfair right? All those false positives kicking around. And you say the guy who invented the test died before he got a chance to stop the use of this test? That's a damn shame. Poor guy. I wonder if it really was pneumonia as they said ...? Hmm. Now you got me thinking. So let's go back to the treatments. You say there are proven treatments for the virus that can prevent serious illness? That could have stopped both Long Covid and possibly death? Yeah I know some people will die of it anyway and some will have lasting side-effects, but I am talking about the majority of people. I mean, they told us this was a pandemic and all those people that have died. Man, that's a real tragedy.'

The data was tampered with.

'What does that mean?'

They lied about the figures

"Whaa ...? The CDC admitted what? That only 6% of reported Covid deaths were actually from Covid? 6%? And they were mostly over aged eighty and possibly would have died from the flu anyway? Except they wouldn't because for the first year ever, the flu has virtually disappeared GLOBALLY? Wow. And we had all those restrictions and all that panic and fear, based on this data which they admitted was untrue? That's not a pandemic, that's a normal virus like flu or a severe cold. By the way, what *has* happened to flu the past eighteen months? It kinda disappeared off the face of the planet! Geez man, I just don't get it. Why would they lie about the test and prevent people from access to proven treatments, And lie about the number of actual deaths. And also block the views of other scientists and medics who are not involved with the governments? Why? Why would they lie?'

To get us in fear

'Fear of what?'

Of dying and Long Covid.

'So all this to get us into some built up fear mode? Really? For what reason?'

They want us to have a vaccine. They want everyone to have the vaccine.

'But that's okay right? I mean, it's only a vaccine. It's not going to do any harm. It's not like we haven't had vaccines as kids, or to visit some place that has diseases like malaria?'

It's not a vaccine.

'Huh? But they told us it is.'

A vaccine has the live virus in it and stays mainly in the injected area to build our immune system against the virus.

'Yeah I get that, but you are saying this is different. How come? And didn't they already do trials on this before saying it was safe to use?'

They have tried for years to produce a SARS-1 vaccine for humans but it kept failing.

'Well how did they know it was failing?'

All the animals in the trials died.

'Blimey, that's not good eh? But this SARS-2 vaccine is different though isn't it? They ironed out the kinks so it was safe to use on humans?'

That's not true. They used mainly the same research to produce the SARS-2 mRNA vaccines as the SARS-1 and yet that killed all the animals in the trial.

'How? What happened to them?'

They responded well for the first few months then their own cells deteriorated and they died. They call it 'antibody dependent enhancement'.

'So you are telling me that the vaccine works for a few months, providing some immunity from the virus, but then it wears off and then may cause the cells in our body to malfunction? Arrghh. I'm beyond confused and a not a little scared. I thought the spike proteins in the vaccine were doing us good?'

The spike proteins that they inject into us, are artificial and were made in a laboratory ready for this pandemic.

'Huh? How can that happen? This virus came out of nowhere right?'

Do the research.

'But I can't be bothered truthfully. I just want an easy life. Okay, you can stop laughing now. Tell me about the spike proteins.'

Millions of these tiny things called spike proteins go into our body via the injection.

'And that then gives us protection against the virus? Gives us immunity against any nasties coming our way right?'

No

'Huh? Hang on, I thought that's why we got the bloody vaccine shot — to give us antibodies to protect us from Coronaviruses? And you're saying it doesn't. Oh man. I am so fricking confused right now.

Okay, okay, take me back to the injection and walk me through it.'

The jab goes into the shoulder but doesn't stay there like normal vaccines would. Only a small percentage, like around 15-20% stays in that area.

'So where do these spike proteins go then if they don't sit in there like good defence soldiers?'

Into your blood circulation.

'Wait … I didn't think they could do that? Or should do that. Well what happens when they go into the circulation system then?'

The lipid nanoparticles that house the spike protein, pretty much go where they shouldn't in the body and build up around the cells.

'Is that okay? Does that help the cell fight the virus?'

No.

'It doesn't? Whaaa …? I don't understand. What do these spike proteins do then and what happens to the cells they stick to? Hang on, I'm doubled vaxxed, do I want to know? No it's okay, don't stop. You've started now and if I'm going to implode or grow another head, I wanna know. No, I'm not laughing. I'm deadly serious, I really do wanna know!'

The spike proteins travel around the body and clump up together and congregate in certain parts of the body.

'Which parts?'

The heart, blood system, the spleen, the brain?

'Arrghh!!! Anywhere else?'

The ovaries and testes?

'Really? Why?'

Good question.

'Man, that doesn't sound good! So let's get this straight. The testing is inaccurate. There are treatments out there that can prevent death and severe illness from this virus, but we aren't allowed access to them. Any medics, lawyers or scientists offering a different viewpoint are de-bunked, barred, silenced or lose their jobs and their social media accounts often shut down. They lied about the number of cases and deaths from this virus to make it look like a pandemic but it isn't really? We are coerced by a regime of fear to take a vaccine you say isn't really a vaccine but an experimental drug that has never been tested on humans before. And then to top it all off, it seems the very cure we are told to take to prevent something that can be treated with something we aren't allowed to have, could likely end up causing us more severe problems to our body, or even death, than the virus itself? And I'm supposed to be okay with this?'

You didn't listen before.

'What do you mean I didn't listen before? You only just told me!'

We told you, but you wouldn't listen.

'We were told before? By whom? Those crazy conspiracy theorists? Come on ... nobody listens to them!'

COERCION

Sounds a bit like Venetian,

a really regal sounding word,

but coercion isn't regal,

now get a grip you crazy bird!

Coercion's a bit like persuading,

but a much less sweeter pill.

It's really making you do some stuff,

against your thought and against your will.

Propaganda's like coercion,

that can lead to the same outcome,

but I much prefer to use my nod,

so stick coercion up yer bum!

MAN ON TOP OF A MOUNTAIN

There's a man who sits atop a mountain. A funny looking little man with a funny little voice and beady, distrusting eyes. A man who knows a lot behind that smirk of a smile.

He doesn't sit on that mountain by himself though, he is simply part of a mountain goat brigade of similar thinking men, overlooking the world they have created beneath them. Everything is beneath them. That's why they sit on top of the mountain.

This man has many fingers in many pies. It's what he does. He has fingers in pies. In fact, he creates the pies and simply stretches his fingers, which seem to grow as time goes by, into more and more fingers, which end up in more and more pies.

Funny thing fingers in pies. Dirty little skinny computer tech fingers that have never grafted in sun or lay for hours in grime soaked gloves. Dirty fingers sitting in inedible pies. Pies made for others to enjoy, but always a huge slice offered back. He has many slices of many pies. Far too many to eat, but then eating pies isn't his thing. He is way above the world for that. The world thinks of him as a great and honourable man. Helping others through his pie offerings. But alas, little do they know that the pies are actually his, because he has fingers in them and that his charitable heart is not quite as charitable as one is led to believe. Funny thing pies and fingers and fingers in pies.

He may be a little lonely on his particular part of the mountain though. His female goat has up and left. Gone through some other mountain *gate* perhaps? Why or where to is questionable, but there are always more questions than understandable answers these days.

Ah that man who sits above the mountain surveying the land he has amassed. Land with no cattle, just a lot of sheep. However, like the cattle, the sheep will soon be culled.

Oh to be a man on top of a mountain with his fingers in his pies, counting his sheep one by one until there is no more than just the one.

JUST A SPOONFUL OF MIDAZOLAM

Poor old little Grandma,
she paid her lifelong dues,
she sold her house and packed her bags,
to move into someplace new.

She had a little room,
though it didn't have a view.
She didn't really mind,
for she was way past ninety-two.

Then one day little ole Grandma,
with her achy breaky bones,
found she felt real poorly,
along with many others in her Home.

She took herself to bed
and told she had to take,
a spoonful of some weird stuff,
that in a lab in France was made.

They didn't tell her fam,
or any of her friends.
Instead they said poor old Grandma
I don't think she will mend.

She couldn't get her breath,
her lungs they wouldn't work,
and every time she tried to talk,
her body gave a jerk.

Goodbye little ole Grandma,
you lived a life so swell,
but death it shouldn't have happened,
it wasn't your time to ring that bell.

THE YELLOW BRICK ROAD

Are you getting the picture yet? Are you seeing what you are being shown? That all is not so well in the land of Oz if you followed the Yellow Brick Road. The magical Wizard you were promised is simply an illusion to pacify you into submission. Life really is like living in The Truman Show.

But hey, don't despair; don't be blue. Didn't Dorothy figure out a way to get home? Okay, she may have had to face the Wicked Witch and melt her into a smoking puddle, but she got to keep those beautiful red sparkly shoes! And Truman finally figured out the lie and found the exit door, despite the storms and tribulations thrown at him just beforehand.

Take heart. You know the truth. The answers are inside you; they have always been there. You simply chose to forget.

Can you blame yourself for accepting the lie? Isn't life so much easier when you go 'yeah sure, whatever,' than standing up and fighting against the go with it tide? No one can blame you for swallowing the tosh they gave you. They play the game so well. And they had the advantage of having created it after all, so how the heck are you getting a fair chance of winning? You aren't! You are always going to play right into their hands. After all, you're the Squid and this is their game.

But now you know. Now it's not so easy because you have lifted off the veil, opened your eyes and swallowed a different colour pill. The world is not quite as joyful, innocent and colourful as it was yesterday is it?

But you are free. And life is what you make of it after all.

What would happen if you chose not to see, not to take off the veil and not to open your eyes? Could your life stay this sweet and relatively nonchalant forever? Hmm. Shall we take a hypothetical look? A snippet of what could be? Just for fun you know, just for fun ...

You didn't lift the veil.

You chose not to see.

You preferred not to know.

Welcome to your future life. Let's exclude annihilation and eugenics here for one moment. Let's face it, it's ugly and depressing and what's coming is ugly enough ...

You get a booster because the variants keep attacking everyone and the booster is sold to you as a way of fighting the variants. They tell you the kids and teens are the super spreaders and since you are so hooked up into the fear propaganda and you are watching your double jabbed friends and family falling sick or even worse, dying from these variants, that you sign your kids up willingly.

The unvaxxed, the great unwashed are being accused of being 'petri dishes for the variants.' Despite many of these not getting sick and forgetting that you too were once the unvaxxed before you got the vax, and that if you do not take the booster and then the following booster, you will also be classed as un-vaxxed, you do not flinch when they are segregated and relieved that they are distanced from you. People you once knew, friends, family, start to disappear. You don't say anything because you are so bought into the narrative and caught up in the web of fear and lies, that you feel they kinda got what they deserved.

Yet even with the unvaxxed disappearing, still the variants rip through your nation, hospitalising many and filling the morgues to the brim. Who is there left to blame? The teens are being forced to have it and so it's the younger kids and the babies. So you allow them to have it. In fact, you are one of the people screaming for mandatory jabs for everyone, including the babies!

More people get sick and die. You are told that you all need another booster to fight the viruses. They keep mutating into different variants. You have already had every brainwave variant. You start to wonder if they've covered all the names of the countries and states yet? What are the next set of variants going to be called?

You are back in lockdown. You went into one in winter and have yet to emerge. Society is crumbling. People are sick and dying; not just from Covid, but from untreated cancer and other diseases and from suicides, murders and robberies. Society as it falls apart is heading into anarchy. There are continual food and supply shortages. Supermarket shelves are bare. People fight in the street and fight for queues to the food banks. There are so few supplies to go round. Vehicle fuel is expensive and in demand and stock is low. Another reason for anarchy.

Soon the babies and the young get sick, but the hospitals aren't accepting new patients. they are crushed to capacity. And there is not enough staff since they sacked those who refused the jab. You are unable to help or save your child. Your grief and starvation and constant fight for survival crush your soul. You want to fight, but you are tied into a Chinese style social credit system that will penalise or reward your every move. They brought in an ID system after the passports. You didn't oppose the vaccine passports because your 'I'm alright Jack' thinking at the time made you ambivalent of the consequences. Besides, you were desperate for a holiday and would have sold your granny to get abroad.

And that's what you did. You sold your granny to a lonely death in a care home. They quietly euthanized her with Midazolam and told you it was Covid. No one questioned it. You sold your kid to a lifelong heart condition caused by a reaction to the vaccine when they had virtually no chance of getting the virus anyway. Not even your favourite footballers collapsing or dying on the pitch was warning enough for you. You sold your allegiance to the friends and family who didn't get the jab and called them selfish. 'They get what they deserve,' you told yourself as you watched them being taken away or live on food banks and on the fringes of society, because they had no access to money or to the stores.

You sold your long term health prospects because you wanted to fit in and because you believed your sacrificial double injection and subsequent booster shots were 'for the good of society.' You even displayed a blue badge proudly on your social media accounts.

You fitted in. Good for you. How's that new normal working out?

There is a Yellow Brick Road. There is a meadow with lots of flowers. The Tin Man wants a heart; the Lion wants to find courage and the Straw Man, well apart from a brain, he just wants to be loved. The Wicked Witch wants to stop you finding your way home. She'll do anything to distract you or prevent you from figuring it all out. The lovely Witch from the West is always encouraging you to open your eyes and trust her. Can you trust her though? Or are you going to follow the Yellow Brick Road to find the Wizard who will get you all the things he promised? A holiday, a return to normal, a hug from granny and all of this nasty pandemic stuff to just simply go away?

Just remember, that there isn't really a Wizard. Just a scamming old man playing tricks behind a theatrical curtain.

BUT the tin man got his ticking heart, the lion already had the courage before he got the certificate to prove it and the straw man ... well, didn't everyone just love him anyway, with or without his brain? And as for Dorothy and Toto ... she just had to visualise her home and it all manifested itself.

There really isn't a Wizard you know, but there is a Yellow Brick Road. How long you gonna keep walking it till you figure out a different path home?

PSYOPS

'Sir, the Plan is well underway.'

'The people don't suspect a thing?'

'Only the conspiracy theorists but nobody believes anything they say anyway.'

'Yeah, we did a good job on them before all this. Gotta love a bit of warm up psyops on that lot.'

The two men start laughing and pat each other on the back.

'I must say sir, that this is truly a brilliant plan. In fact, the way the people have bought it so easily; it's bloody genius!'

'Why thank you comrade. It was nothing. No, I mean it, it was nothing. Simply a little mass mind control through a propaganda of fear and discombobulating information. It was really very simple.'

'Forgive me sir, but HOW did you get them to succumb so quickly? I mean it took just months before they started to give up their rights and freedoms. It was just so simple.'

'Well comrade, don't forget that this has been decades of planning. We tried it a few times before don't forget!'

'Yes but this sir, this is incredible. The whole world has succumbed. Genius, pure genius.'

'We almost lost them a couple of times, but you cannot underestimate the power of fear. Tell them there's a pandemic and a virus that could either kill or leave a person with long term side effects and you have them pretty much eating out of your hands. First you create the chaos, then you offer the cure. That way you are bringing order out of chaos. On one hand we create the chaos and in the other we say, 'here you go, here's the cure!' Bloody ace!'

Again the two start chuckling as they sat with their coffees in their secret meeting place.

'But why do they succumb? That's the bit I am interested in. How was it so easy to get them to do what we wanted?'

'Well comrade, we used every resource we had. The media was the biggest player throughout. First was the catastrophe — the outbreak of a virus. Yeah we made up the story about the Chinese market place, but if we told them it was deliberately leaked from a US funded laboratory in China with links to a US university and US government and that the virus was meant to be much more dangerous than the one that did leak, then I am pretty sure it wouldn't have had the same impact, do you?'

'No, I guess not. Especially if the people of the world found out about the links to Fauci, Gates and the US leadership. Man, that was clever to say that stuff about the bat and the wet market. It was so out there, that I was sure the people would see through it!'

'Comrade, remember this ... if you tell someone an outright lie, but you do it with a straight face and it comes out as truth, then they are not really going to question it. Especially if it's coming from credible sources like the media, the military and of course, the leaders of their country.'

'Sir that is indeed a genius plan. The whole thing, from start to now, is incredible. Geez.'

The two men took a moment to sip on their coffee, bite into their pastry and sit back and reflect. The older, more senior in rank man spoke first.

'They say it takes twenty-one days to change a habit. Well, we locked the world down for weeks and months. We got them used to being out of the system. I suppose you could say, we broke them out of their routines. That was their 'old normal.' Then we imposed rules and restrictions on them. Some were imposed immediately and some we introduced along the way. We got them used to being told what to do. We told them not to wear masks, so they didn't. Then we told them they had to wear them and stand two metres away from each other. They complied. It was so darn easy from then on to carry out the rest of the Plan. They were already complying to the rules, even when they didn't make any sense and were contradictory.'

'Like sheep being shepherded?'

'Exactly! In fact, it's ironic that those who rebel, call the people sheep.'

'I heard that they call them 'Sheeple'! It's hilarious when you think about it. That's exactly what they are.'

Again the two men chuckle. The senior man continued.

'Once they were programmed to follow orders, it was simple. The media, governments, institutions, medical facilities, scientists and legal systems around the world, were all instructed to sell the same story. And the people, simply followed the narrative. Trusting whatever they were being told as though their lives depended on it. Oh wait ... they really did think their lives depended on it! Hah!'

'What I don't understand,' said the younger man, 'is why they didn't react when they found out the data on number of cases and deaths was incorrect, or when it was exposed that the PCR test wasn't accurate, given that was the main diagnosis for cases to be recorded. And then all that stuff about the Gates Foundation, child trafficking, Epstein Island, suspicious deaths of presidents and top CEO's opposed to the Plan, plus Dr. Fauci and his ineptness and those goddamn exposing emails! I mean, it's all there in black and white; all the evidence of something not being quite right; it's all there. But the people, or should I say, the *Sheeple*, don't do ANYTHING!'

'Yes, it amazes me too comrade, but you have to remember the power of propaganda and especially the propaganda of fear over people. Do not underestimate the power of the psychological warfare that we have been imposing on the people for generations. The foundations were laid so that these lies could be ingested as truth. That's why it was so simple. Take Nazi Germany for example. How easy was it for Hitler and the Nazi regime to convince the German people that the Jews were the enemy of the world? It didn't take long before they succumbed to that way of thinking. Some of these Germans and Jews were best friends! By the time we were finished with the Germans, they were convinced the Jews needed to be destroyed and exterminated. Psyops my friend, is one of the most powerful tools in our bag!'

'So what now? Now we have them penned in, what are we going to do with the Sheeple?'

'Well, we are giving them a summer of relief. Thanking them for getting doubled jabbed, by re-instating some, if not most of their freedoms. And whilst they are booking holidays, eating out and partying, the resistance to the Plan, the unvaxxed, well, we do to them what we did to the Jews in Germany — we create a division; a segregation. At this point, the double jabbed are starting to get sick or die unexpectedly. Fear is building once again and they have no idea it's because of the very medicine they took to protect them from falling sick in the first place! By the time summer is over, the double vaxxed will see the unvaxxed as the enemy. And that's when the Plan really kicks in.'

'See that's what I was wondering sir, in Nazi Germany, the Jews were different, because of their religion and culture. It was easy then to segregate them in society, just as it has always been with people of black origin. But the unvaxxed could be anyone — a neighbour, a friend, a family member, a partner. How are we going to convince the vaxxed that these people that walk beside them, are their enemy?'

'Good question comrade. It seems incredible to us, but the answer is that they will simply believe whatever we tell them. We have already proven that they do not question the narrative, so why, with 'normality' being in the grasp of their hands, are they going to let it go now, to save a friendship, a cousin, a neighbour, or even their own child or spouse? People are selfish. Ultimately, they only care about what's best for them.'

'Whilst all the time being told it's for the greater good of society eh?'

'Exactly comrade. Exactly.'

'So what are we going to do with the unvaxxed then?'

'First we must definitely introduce mandatory child vaccinations. We want all the children vaxxed so we can continue with the Greater Plan. As we know, the spike proteins affect the reproductive organs, thus reducing the number of people being born in the future. Then we start taking the unvaxxed away. They will have the choice of course. Mandatory vaccination laws will be passed and those not complying will simply disappear.'

'Such a truly brilliant plan sir. Brilliant. Well done, I must congratulate you and your men. As I said before, it has been so easy, despite the obvious hiccups. But I must say that I thought man would offer more resistance you know? I really didn't think people would be so compliant and so malleable. Especially when you think of how intelligent man is. It still amazes me sir, how easy it has been.'

'That comrade, is the power of a propaganda operation. We convinced the people that their lives were in danger and thus they would do anything to survive. Do not underestimate man's desire to live rather than die. If they thought they could survive a deadly pandemic, then they would literally sell their granny to do so. Oh wait ... many of them did!'

The two men laughed so hard that the younger man started to cough uncontrollably. A piece of pastry hadn't quite managed to make its way into his digestion system and was loitering around the back of his throat. The older man stopped laughing and with a serious face questioned his companion.

'Coughing is the sign of a virus comrade! We'd better get you checked out!'

The younger man stopped coughing and went pale. He felt the icy cold vein of fear chill his blood.

Then the older man laughed again.

'You should have seen your face comrade! See? See how easy it is to install fear into someone? And you even know it's a lie!'

Again the two men laughed hard. But the younger man held back just a little and kept a side eye to the older man. In that moment, he knew that even being a part of the Plan did not keep him entirely safe.

WHAT IF

What if we are wrong? For one minute, just imagine that we are wrong and that ...

— The virus wasn't man made from a laboratory in China funded by the US to create a new form of bio weapon.

— They hadn't patented both the virus and vaccine years ago. Why would they do that?

— Dr. Fauci really did have our best interests at heart.

— There weren't existing cures and treatments for the virus already in place that could prevent long term Covid effects and death, but they were barred from use because they weren't part of the 'Plan'.

— That Vitamin D, Zinc and high doses of Vitamin C aren't natural boosts for the immune system and anyone posting this at the beginning of the 'pandemic', hadn't had their posts taken down by fact checkers as false information.

— That fact checkers weren't in cahoots with the pharmaceutical companies.

— That this health information mentioned above, would not have prevented a lot of people getting very poorly and or dying.

— That it isn't in the pharmaceutical companies' best interests to keep us hooked on their drugs and vaccines.

— That they weren't making a shit load of dough from vaccinating us.

— That the world's global elite; the world's top richest men and women and the vaccine producing pharmaceutical companies didn't increase their income exponentially during the pandemic.

— That you actually cared that humanity's distress over the past eighteen months, has been exploited by a minority of the world's wealthiest people.

— That they were so caring for our health that the pharmaceutical companies did not agree to be without reprehension or liability if God forbid, their vaccines did more harm than good.

— They hadn't disbarred, discredited and debunked hundreds and thousands of eminent and credible doctors, scientists and lawyers globally who did not agree with their narrative.

— They allowed freedom of speech and different perspectives on the current situation.

— Doctors aren't threatened with imprisonment for either speaking out or using alternative, proven treatments, including holistic and naturopath treatments.

— Presidents of countries refusing to comply, CEO's of multi million pound businesses threatening to expose, directors of films highlighting an alternative truth, haven't been murdered (including their wife, young children and dog) or coincidentally, just died.

— That they didn't create a propaganda of fear and lie about data and statistics to sustain the fear that this is a deadly, difficult to treat virus pandemic.

— The vaccines were real vaccines that protect you and build your immune system instead of destroying the very immune system they profess it to support.

— That the spike protein doesn't cling to the cells in your blood system and kill the body's natural immune defence T Cells.

— That every type of virus your body now encounters won't be more dangerous because the army of natural defence T Cells have been compromised.

— That each extra booster shot doesn't swarm the body with more of the T Cell killing artificial spike proteins.

— That antibody dependent enhancement (ADE) wasn't a thing.

— That the vaccine isn't part of a developed bio weapon plan by a globalist elite who want to reduce the world's population by at least 50%.

— That there wasn't a globalist elite group that has infiltrated every part of society and has been planning this for decades.

— That World Economic Forum Founder Klaus Schwab didn't already tell us what they planned in his book The Great Reset.

— The Georgia Stones aren't the outlines for a new world Plan by a global elite group Deep State

— That there isn't a Deep State.

— That there isn't a Plan for a New World Order, one Global Government, a cashless society and to ID micro-chip every person on the planet.

— That the leaders of the world and anyone in power or in royalty, have not all been saying 'Build Back Better' since the very beginning of the 'pandemic'.

— That I did not just ask you to ask yourself why?

— That the damage to nature and the climate that the New World Order talks about limiting, they have also been a part of with their associations to the very businesses exploiting nature and the climate.

— That geo-engineering doesn't exist and definitely not affecting our weather systems.

— That geo-engineering is not punching the crap out of our ozone layer and thus creating climate damage.

— That many past and present global leaders did not meet in a secret elite club whilst students at a top US University (Skull and Bones/ Yale).

— That 'the old boy network' exists in the most extreme sense of the word and that kindness for the majority of humanity is not at the top of their agenda.

— That this globalist elite do not see the majority of humanity as 'useless feeders' that need to be gotten rid of or controlled.

— That humanoids were not a plan for the coming future and that there was not information on government websites relating to this.

— That they didn't have the ability to alter the structure of the human DNA with lipid nanoparticle technology, never before injected into humans.

— That the mRNA vaccines do not have this nano technology as an ingredient.

— That a global court did not rule that whoever owned the patent of the bio technology that affects the cell's DNA, did not then own the subject with the technology in their DNA. Think about that one ...

— That the mRNA vaccines do not have carcinogenic ingredients.

— That the ingredients in the mRNA vaccines had previously been combined together and been tested on humans. The animals they were tested on did not all die.

— That some of the humans in the global trials did not get severe side effects or indeed suffer death as a result.

— That they actually did the initial trials on a huge number of people instead of only a handful of humans and that they did not exclude children, expectant mothers, those with diseases like cancer or anyone with a suppressed or compromised immune system.

— That many of the children they did test on did not suffer extreme reactions and even death and that there is a robust compensation in place for vaccine trial humans suffering side effects or death as a result of the trials.

— That they were not developed via testing on human embryos and that some of them do not have human embryo parts as an ingredient.

— That one of the ingredients of the vaccine is not called Luciferase which is not a bioluminescence and probably has absolutely nothing to do with a tracking implementation in the recipient's body.

— That child trafficking does not exist.

— That Hollywood, Disney, the upper layers of society and politics, are not associated or not aware of those associated with child trafficking.

— That underground tunnels to traffic and house babies and children for sexual, ritual sacrifice and unethical purposes do not exist.

— That Epstein Island wasn't a thing and that Pizzagate did not involve some of those people whom you love in politics and on TV.

— That a politician ordering a pizza was really just about a politician ordering a pizza.

— That eight million children do not go missing each year, often without investigation.

— That you could not buy human embryos and body parts online.

— That you could not buy children online via top shopping sites.

— That adrenochrome is not the secretion of blood from the adrenal gland of a traumatised young child. That the more they scream in fear, the greater the adrenaline running through the blood and thus creating a more lucrative secretion for the recipient.

— That the drug of choice for the rich and famous wasn't Adrenochrome, otherwise known as the Luciferian drug.

— That these people didn't believe that the blood of the young was an anti-ageing tool for themselves.

— That taking one dose of the vaccine was enough.

— That the vaccine didn't only provide six months immunity therefore leaving the vaccinated not just immune compromised, but also requiring booster vaccines to flood your immune with even more T Cell killing spike proteins.

— That it wasn't true that the more spike proteins in your body, the greater chance of negative effects on your body.

— That cykotine storm wasn't a thing.

— That the very dangerous to humans ingredient Graphene Oxide wasn't being used in the vaccines at a high dose, toxic level and that it was simply a beautiful ingredient to benefit the human body.

— That you would not sell out your granny, your neighbour, your lifelong friend, your cousin, your parent, your spouse, your child, because they told you to.

— That they cared about us and only want to protect us and that they have our best interests at heart.

— That you are not controlled by a propaganda machine that has blinded you to the most endearing parts of being a human being — love of others, kindness, honesty, charitable heart, reason, understanding, fairness, emotional intelligence.

— That you will not wake up soon and realise that you are being led quietly and silently to the slaughterhouse 'for the greater good'.

We so hope we are wrong. We really do. But what if we are right?

LOSING FAITH

That's what they want, us to lose faith in our truth so that we give in. Offering us free donuts, lottery tickets, money, fries and other bribery delectable stuff, just so we would not take our time and wait to make a balanced decision on whether to take the jab or not.

They haven't let us breathe, or given us time to think, so we could make a balanced choice. They closed the bars and restaurants, the churches and places of worship and any area where we might congregate to share opinions, discuss and have conversation about the pros and cons of having it verses waiting. The coercion tactics were so strong that it was easier to just give in.

They opened up vaccination centres at fast food outlets, theme parks, restaurants, churches, community centres. Places they closed for socialising and community conversations, they opened for the purpose of injecting us with an unknown combination of medical substances. And one dose suddenly wasn't enough. It had to be two before we were included into the 'acceptable club' of the first tier in society. Now a third and then a fourth, a fifth and so on. And we so love to fit in.

What if we stop at two and don't take up the booster, or the next booster, or the one after that? Will we move down a rung into 'almost acceptable' or down further with the one or no jab brigade and be totally ostracised? Have we really sunk this low?

It would be easy to lose faith; to give up on our individuality; to just do as we are asked. But then what? What happens then? At what point do we step back and say the following ...

'Enough! I've done what you asked of me. I've stayed home, closed my business, didn't go to work, didn't see friends or family. I wore a mask, didn't touch anyone and treated everyone I met like a walking virus spreader. I went back to the bars, the restaurants and paid the inflated prices because I know they need to earn back what they lost. I took my first dose, ignored the pain in my arm, the sweats, the shakes, the palpitations, the flu-like symptoms, the days in bed, the headaches, eye aches. I toed the line. I went for my second jab despite being nervous after the first. I got my certificate and duly posted my jabbed status on my social media walls.

I'm a good citizen. I did my bit for the greater good. I protected the vulnerable and the elderly, despite the fact that they got the jab before me. But I listened and did as the media and the leaders asked. I did it for 'the greater good'.

So why do I feel such a sense of loss? That despite all that I have done, that things will never return to normal? That the new variants are getting people despite all the restrictions and precautions? That there is a desperation in the air?'

Is that you? Are you losing faith? In society, in people, in the leadership, in your Creator? Are you asking yourself how we can get back to where we were before March 2020? Is life beyond weird and confusing and nothing makes sense?

It's all of that and more. Keep your faith. Know who you are. In fact, keep questioning who you are and keep your individuality. Check your morals and your ethics; have they been compromised lately? Are you starting to think differently? Kinda like a 'them and us' thing? If so, you might want to look closer at that. Remember the words 'divide and conquer'? Once a community or society is divided, it is so much easier to conquer. Take a look at the following story. It might make you think.

THE STORY OF THE ANT AND THE NARROW-MOUTHED TOAD

One day a wee little ant was minding his own business and chewing on a leaf. He had been busy all morning collecting for the colony with his brethren and felt like a well-deserved break was in order. The sun was shining, the birds were away in the trees and all was good in the world of the ant, so he took off by himself to a corner of the forest beside a pond. In fact, he was so busy relaxing and giving thanks for the blessings in his life, that he failed to notice that he was no longer alone.

'Glub, Glub' came a noise from behind him. The ant turned around just in time to see a long, sticky tongue swipe straight past him.

'Hey!' cried out the ant to the narrow-mouthed toad trying to eat him. 'Get lost!'

'Be quiet and get in my tummy!' said the toad in between shooting out his tongue a couple of times to capture his midday snack. He had already feasted on a bunch of sleeping termites, so the ant was kinda like a sweet dessert post lunch. He wasn't happy about his food talking back either, so he was quite determined to capture the little critter.

'Hah! Missed again! What are you, some kind of fat slobbery wuss?' The ant was quite a brave, albeit impudent creature.

The toad grunted then critically laughed.

'How dare you! Do you know who I am?'

The ant, who was actually deciding on whether or not to scarper from the large, slobbery amphibian, stopped to stare at his opponent.

'Yes. You are a big bully who thinks because of your size, that you are more powerful than me.'

The toad, who had never stopped long enough with his food to have a conversation with it, thought for a moment, looking more than a little perplexed. He peered at the tiny little creature who dared to challenge him.

'But little guy, I *am* more powerful than you.'

The ant put his hand to his chin and looked thoughtful.

'Mmm, I can see your point. There is just one of me standing before you and me being so small and you so much bigger, I can see why you think you are so much more powerful than myself.'

The toad laughed. He was thinking of sticking out his tongue and lapping up the ant whilst it was distracted, but he found he was enjoying this rare conversation with his food. Then again, the midday sun was getting hot and he needed some shade. Plus he was beginning to find the conversation a little tedious, so he steadied himself ready to indulge in a little ant snack and be on his way back to the pond.

'I know what you're thinking.' declared the ant all of a sudden. The toad closed his narrow mouth and thought to himself *you do?* 'You are thinking that you will quickly gobble me and be on your way and because I am just one small, insignificant ant, that I will be easy meat to eat.'

'Yes. Indeed you are!' replied the toad with a small, narrow mouthed smile.

'But what if I was an army of ants? What would you do then?' the ant suddenly remarked. The toad noticed that the ant wore a curious smile on his face.

'I guess I would still try to eat all of you and thus would have much more than a tiny ant to snack on. I would have a feast!' declared the toad with an extravagant wave of its little toad arms.

'Could you do that lying on your back with leaves stuffed in your mouth?' asked the ant with a sly smile.

The ant looked curiously at the toad and the toad looked even more curious at the ant. Then the ant stepped to one side just at the point of the toad's tongue flicking out to gobble him up. The tongue did not return empty however, just not attached to a juicy little ant. Instead, was a large bundle of green leaves that filled the tiny mouth of the narrow-mouthed toad.

'Waaa ...' it tried to scream with incredulity as it started to choke on the salad stuck to its tongue. As it struggled to breathe, he felt himself wobble. Some kind of force was pulling him over. *Whack!* He landed with a thump on his back on the ground, with his mouth still full of foul tasting greenery. He wasn't a big salad eater and definitely in no way a vegan.

He lay there as the sun beat down on his less than slimy body. He felt his skin drying and he craved the lush waters of the pond. Despite how he was feeling, his thoughts turned to the ant. What happened? How did he end up in this situation he wondered as panic rose up inside him.

The ant causally wandered to the upturned toad.

'I guess you are wondering right now, how a big toad like you who eats ants every day for breakfast, lunch and dinner, got himself floored by one tiny little ant huh?'

The toad unable to answer, grunted and bulged his eyes. He did indeed want to know.

'Well,' started the ant as he was slowly accompanied by not just one, not just two or three, but hundreds of ants, who casually surrounded the eye bulged, choking toad slowly drying out in the hot midday sun. 'You see, when we met, I was indeed simply one small, innocuous ant who, compared to your size, was at a huge disadvantage. But you see, us ants, despite our size are a unique type of creature.' The ant breathed in and continued, signalling the other ants to his dying opponent. 'You see, individually we can be overwhelmed by giants and those whom we feel are more powerful. But collectively, we are a greater force to be reckoned with. We have a code within our ant society. What happens for one, happens for all. Thus we look out for each other. We work together for the good of the survival of our colony and we stand as brothers and sisters in arms beside one another. Kinda like an 'all for one and one for all' collective mentality.'

The ants all cheered in unison and patted each other on the back. Then they started to leave and return to their work. Break time was indeed over for all. The ant whom the toad initially met as his opportune snack after lunch, walked over to the toad. The ant could see that the other creature's situation was not going to end well for him.

'You may be more powerful when confronted by just one of me, but when we come together as one, we are far more powerful and ingenious than you could ever imagine. All it took was a few leaves, some vine, lots of ant power, some creative thinking and we had a plan.' Then he put his foot over the fat toad's tummy and declared, 'Never underestimate the underdog. We are stronger than you can imagine.' Then he walked off and returned to the others for the afternoon shift in the colony.

The Rise of The Awakened

They came from the east, the west, north and south. They came with a fired up soul and their hearts in their mouths.

With a bellyful of truth and pockets full of knowledge, they came to say no to the lies learned at college.

From the masters and leaders who once held their attention; no to the dark ones that no one will mention.

They started as one, who was asking the question. What, how and when, and why did this happen?

Then one met another and soon there were two, who started to dig and soon there were four. Four turned to ten and ten to a hundred and they multiplied quickly to reach more than a thousand.

All seeking and searching to find out the truth, peeling back layers, exposing stains underneath.

One after another a lie was unfold; stories of fables, some young, some ancient, some old.

Where did it start this systemised world, where masters danced puppets and we did as were told?

Now that they know that it just wasn't true, the people cried out in pain and were blue.

As loved ones succumb and fell under their spell, watching them go was like living in hell.

So the rebels who left the Matrix behind, formed closer bonds to the ones at their side. And like soldiers together, they marched freedom's beat, with light in their hearts and truth under their feet.

Now millions, stood as a unified band, singing and marching to the beat of one drum. And out of the ashes of humanity's fall, a new civilisation rose, with hope their main call.

For they refuse to burn in the wicked ones' fire, or succumb to the greed for money and power. And out of the ashes of humanity's fall, a new civilisation rose; freedom, hope, peace and love, for one and for all.

THE CHILD CATCHER

He doesn't wear black, or have a brightly covered up cage. He doesn't offer candy sweets or sing songs about lollipops, pastries and sugary treats. His nose is indeed crookedly long and his eyes are tiny and pinched as though they were an after-thought addition post creation.

This nefarious human, devoid of the goodness of humanity, is indeed out to capture your children. But alas, there is no cage to transport them to the underground workings of a castle to hide from child hating rulers of a lonely kingdom. Instead, the Child Catcher has a greater, more ridiculous plan.

He wants to medicate them.

And the medicine is bitter and if the kid doesn't like fries or donuts, then they are pretty much stuffed! Nothing healthy is being offered.

The Child Catcher is clever though. He knows that given a choice, the kids wouldn't take the medicine. Because despite their junior years, kids know they aren't sick, so why would they need a medicine? And don't most kids hate taking medicines?

So the Child Catcher tells the parents and the adults around them that if the kids don't take the medicine, the adults could all die of a disease the kids probably will never get, but the adults could, so they should save the adults and stuff the kids!

But wait! What if ...

The Child Catcher was actually using the candy tempting cage to entice the adults to entice the children, because in order to get the children, they first require the complicity of the adults?

Could you imagine?

Oh dear, what a complicated system the Child Catcher has in place. But oh so very devious and clever. What type of character would he be, to even consider such a despicable plan? Is he not like a pied piper playing his narrative tune, in order to lead them to a designated centre where all of the peoples, men, women and children, become medicated 'for the greater good of society?'

So then, based on that assumption, is the Child Catcher not a great and honourable man saving rather than destroying mankind? Surely there is no cause to condemn or criticise if this were the case?

If this were the case, then yes. Give the Child Catcher a medal, an honour, an award, a certificate, a darn hard pat on the back.

If this were the case. But it isn't, is it?

The medicine is not good for the children. It will not necessarily prevent them from getting sick or making others sick. It could however, make them very poorly for simply having taken it. So the Child Catcher still has to convince the children that the medicine is in their best interests to take. Children for the most part however, are pretty clever and they have a sixth sense on many things, including seeing through the cloak of the stranger who offers them candies in the playground. And after all, their parents drummed into them that they should NEVER EVER accept candy from a stranger in the playground.

So the only way the Child Snatcher can make the children take the medicine, is to give the spoon to the parents and ask them to persuade the children that they really should take the medicine, because it's in the best interests of their parents.

Despite the rather gnarly, cold, untrustworthy and rather evil looking appearance of this nefarious Child Catcher, the children cannot say no to protecting granny or perhaps their immune compromised parents or teacher. So they take the medicine.

And with his job done, the Child Snatcher locks up his cage, puts the candies back in their box and heads home to his medicine free family. After all, everyone knows that you shouldn't bring your work home with you.

LET'S TALK LIFE INSURANCE

Let me tell you a story about life insurance. Sitting comfortable? Got your drink handy? Okay, let's begin ...

Did you know that death is a mighty big business? Yup, that's what we said, a mighty big business indeed!

Makes sense right? After all, if there's one thing for certain, we are all going to die one day! Of course, the majority of us don't know when that day will come and we mostly always can't control it. But what if controlling our death was something that made a lot of businesses and individuals a shite load of money?

Did you know that life insurance companies made a tonne of money from all those men who died in World War One? How? Well, everyone got life insurance, but those widows and grieving mommas didn't really understand the process of claiming on their loved ones policies and nobody was helping them with that part of their grief, so they mostly didn't. That's a lot of money banked right there.

Now that may not be huge news, but think for a moment ... what if there were some pretty unscrupulous individuals who realised in the early 1900s say, that death could be so profitable? Hey, we all want to be profitable, so you could say, *'well what's the big deal if some guys create some companies to benefit from people dying, if they were also beneficial to the person who purchased one of their policies?'*

I'm so glad you asked ...

What if (we like those two words; gets you thinking, you know) these individuals did *not* have other people's best interests at heart and were only in it for the bottom, top and heck, the middle line too?

And what if, those big players in the life insurance industry, were also involved in scientific laboratories and medical institutions and some of their work involved developing vaccines?

And what if they were also in cahoots with some of the world's nefarious global elite? Interesting thoughts huh?

We are not going to do this work for you. Apologies. But if we were you, we might be asking at this point ... who benefits from the early death of millions of people? When do life insurance policies pay out? Is your life insurance still viable if you have taken an experimental concoction of drugs not yet FDA approved for regulatory use as a vaccine?

Hmm. All those annuities taken out years ago; wonder if there's still money in the kitty left to pay out? What do you think?

While you're at it, ask if there's enough money in the pot to pay the pensions of those wanting to retire in the next few years? It may be gossip, but we heard there wasn't.

But heck, we're just planting a seed. You want that plant to grow, you gotta water it yourself.

After all, who wants to entertain a conspiracy theory these days? It's not like any of them are coming true or anything now is it?

THE NEW WORLD ORDER

We're going to tell you an old story. It's old because it goes back a very, very long time ago.

First we had Man and some of the men were influenced by Lucifer. Now this ole devil knew man's weakness for power, control and financial gain. So he showed them his plan and filled their pockets with gold and their hearts with stones.

Now we are going to tell you something that might shock you, if you haven't already been shocked enough by the content in this book so far.

Humanity has always been at war. And it's not like any war you have every experienced.

This is a war of dominance and control and power. And to baffle you even more, it's a secret war that maligns itself in the darkest corners of the globe.

Confused? Let's take you back a bit to set the scene.

When a human is born it is free. Then once it has a birth certificate, it is stamped and assigned to being a Ward of the State it is born and registered in. He or she now belongs to a place and becomes the property of that State. Following so far? It gets more interesting herein.

There exists an underlying global control group, called the New World Order, or NWO for short, and they have constructed three ongoing wars — shipping, postal and banking. In the shipping war, a person born into the world becomes what they call 'cargo'. Pretty far-fetched right? Let me explain further.

There exists in this infrastructure, a Post Master General of the World. And according to the Law of the Sea, this is the King/Queen of Great Britain. He or she, is the reigning monarch of the world. Tied into this infrastructure, are all the courts in the world. Thus entire systems are set up for us not to win, because globally, the courts are all connected.

Also in London, are based the thirteen banking families of the world, with the Rothschilds family/empire being the most well-known and highest in profile.

What is fascinating, is how this global elite group of people, tried to control the US Constitution for decades and almost succeeded in 1999, but their plans were foiled. However, they have never given up.

Four US Presidents - Roosevelt, Eisenhower, John F Kennedy and Ronald Reagan, all stood up against this nefarious secret group of influential individuals and families who wanted to create a New World Order. They tried to get Roosevelt out of Office, attempted to assassinate Reagan and successfully assassinated Kennedy, who had managed to set up the Special Forces to combat them.

Meanwhile, the CIA, which was run by George Bush Senior, established the 5 Star Trust. This is the largest drug and money laundering operation ever seen. It is a conglomerate banking system that also involves the Post Master General of GB and the thirteen banking families.

Despite Reagan's warnings about the NWO, George Bush Senior wins office and gets into power. At this point, there are trillions of dollars in the 5 Star Trust, but despite this, they are talking about placing a United Nations tax on people to build their coffers even more. Needless to say, the UN aren't the good guys either. Bush also planned to surrender the US constitution and the flag to GB.

What they wanted to create was so close — a One World Government.

However, to achieve this, they first had to control the military. What they needed, was an orchestrated catastrophic event to indicate that a war on terror was required. Cue the Twin Towers collapse of 9/11. Despite this pointing at being an inside job and not an act of terrorism as the world was led to believe, the military were tricked into thinking that an enemy of the country existed.

Still with us?

So, with Bush Senior in power, who was a member of the Masonic Highest Order of the 33 Group and a University of Yale Skull and Bones member (look these up — Masonic Lodge elitism), the NWO were on target for achieving their goal of a global One World Government, with the world and all of humanity under its' control.

Meanwhile, there were nine banking systems not under the control of the Rothschilds and the banking families empire. Seven of these were in the Middle East. Thus, Bush and his group of global pirates, decided that they should go to war with each of these countries and take down their governments. The plan was to start with Iraq, then Syria, followed by Lebanon, Libya, Sudan and Iran. Finally, they would take down Venezuela.

They would go to the Middle East, steal their gas and oil and overtake their banks. These were to be manufactured wars for the sole purpose of creating more wealth and power and to continue the plan of establishing a One World Government. And remember, that their allegiance is not to God or the wellbeing of humanity as a whole!

But alas, they had not accounted for the heroic actions of two men - Russell J Gould and David-Wynn Miller. In 1999, Gould managed to salvage the US flag and the Constitution so that it would not be lost to GB and ultimately under the control of the NWO. Out of this came the US Bill of Rights.

After 1999, George Bush Junior, also a 33 group and Skull and Bones member and part of the NWO, wins office. 9/11 happens and he starts a war on Iraq.

Then came Obama who pushed for people to buy private health care, which ties them to the life insurance companies and the pharmaceutical industry. Now there is Biden, Harris and Nancy Pelosi placed exactly where they can use them. Oh and don't forget the Clintons, Epstein Island and all those very expensive pizzas going on there. If you don't understand the pizzas, maybe you should look into the Epstein story a little more. And don't forget the little boy emerging from the underground tunnels in the story 'The Four Leaf Clover' earlier on in this book. It's all rather messy isn't it?

So then, why are we telling you all this? Read the next bit with a very open mind and with big seeing eyes.

You see, there is still the desire to set up a one ruling global government. And this government would control the global population as they saw fit. This includes NATO being a global world enforcer, who could destroy people and places in an instant; a United Nations tax on everyone, global trade policies to suit only them, an ID chip inserted into everyone thus removing the requirement for cash, since this chip would hold all our money and data. They will have the power to turn this access to money on or off as they so wish. Everyone will be part of a database and thus become slaves to this government. Freedom as humans as we now know it now, would disappear. It would be a one-size fits all existence, where the individual owns nothing and relies on the NWO for all their basic requirements. We look to them to be fed, watered and housed. And if they decided one day that we are expendable meat, then that feeding tube gets shut down.

Why is this relevant today?

The New World Order has not gone away. They still want a Global Government. They still want a cashless society. They still have the same desire to take away individual freedoms and rights as they always have. They still want to enslave humanity with an ID chip. They still plan to euthanize a large percentage of the world to increase the availability of resources. They adhere to the concept of eugenics.

They are behind the financial, pharmaceutical, technological, medical, scientific, educational, political, media and entertainment industries globally. They will stop at nothing to place what they want into existence.

Think about that for a moment — they will stop at nothing to achieve their goal.

After all, human beings are simply assigned 'cargo' to them.

How's that Yellow Brick Road looking now?

SO NOW WHAT?

Now you know all this, you have a choice. You always have a choice, you know that right? You were born with free will. Perhaps you simply forgot that was in your tool bag? Remember the story of 'The Stream' at the beginning of the book? We were born with free will. We are sovereign beings and have inalienable rights.

If you choose to think that these are all merely conspiracy theories and you are content to go along with saying yes and trusting what you are told, then that is totally your choice. Take your chance and see what life brings your way. You might find that we are talking baloney and none of the bad stuff will happen.

We really pray to God it doesn't. Sometimes, it doesn't help to be right.

But just for one moment, what if we were right and there really does exist a global elitist group carrying out an evil eugenics plan to annihilate and control the planet? What then? Is it too late to save the world; to save yourselves?

Alas, not everyone will be or can be saved. However, we can still stop them. We can save our children and help ourselves. We can simply say *no* and stand up against them. We do not surrender. This is a time to look to our God and to stand in the light of faith. Remember that light will always be stronger than darkness.

Remember the earlier story of the ant and the toad? There is power in numbers. Despite being just one man, Russell J Gould stood up against this NWO. What collectively, could we achieve if we all stood up and took back the power of our destiny? All we have to do is say *'no'*.

Perhaps there is something in the vaccine that is dulling your mind to seeing the truth. Or could it simply be the brainwashing, mind control tactics deployed by the very best psychological operational people in the world? They were actually employed to do this work you know, that really is fact not conspiracy type theories.

Think back before March 2020, if you can. Would you have believed that you would ...

— Willingly give up your freedom.

— Willingly give up your rights.

— Willingly give up your freedom to choose.

— Be coerced into having an injection that had never been tested on a human before and isn't actually classified as a vaccine and only authorised to be used as an emergency drug and on trial until 2023. All the animals they trialled this on died. None survived!

— Not hug your family members or friends for fear of killing them or getting killed by something that has very little chance to kill or seriously harm you or them.

— Willingly allow others to not have life-saving or life changing treatment for other illnesses and diseases, because it frees-up time and availability for the medical institutions to inject you with something that prevents you from getting sick from something you have very little chance of getting seriously sick from.

— Do nothing when informed that the person who told you there was a pandemic, actually funded the laboratory that deliberately created the virus in the first place, who has been involved in patenting and developing vaccines for decades and who also has been involved in the needless death of thousands of HIV victims via the prescription of a deadly drug (Fauci).

— You would not complain when the CDC admitted that only 6% of reported Covid-19 deaths were actually Covid-19 deaths.

— Despite knowing that all of the pharmaceutical companies have had numerous multi-billion dollar damage claims against them because of previous drugs and vaccines, you did not flinch when they bring out a 'rushed through' experimental drug (their official description) they labelled a 'vaccine' not yet approved by the FDA, nor did you blink an eye when they told you that these companies would not be liable for any related damages or deaths caused by taking this non approved experimental drug. Basically, you have no discourse or personal rights if it all goes tits-up!

— You would not complain when you were informed that the PCR testing system, the basis for lockdowns and restrictions, was an inaccurate test? And you don't even flinch when even the inventor of this test says it should not be used as a testing system for a pandemic virus? (and then he dies).

— You would turn your back on family and friends if they chose not to, or could not have this 'vaccine'.

— That you would be crying out for the unvaccinated to be punished in society.

— That you would be prepared to watch your fellow human being: friend or foe, starve, be penalised, beaten up by police, or thrown into prison, for choosing not to be vaccinated.

— That you ignore all the evidence of bots on social media spreading disinformation and propaganda against anyone against the narrative. And that you don't say a word when many so-called 'patients' ill with Covid, shown by mainstream media, are paid actors.

— That you will believe everything you are told without questioning, even when presented with differing information or data that indicates that what you have been told is not the truth.

— That despite information stating children have a very low risk of catching Covid and are not spreaders of the virus, you would happily allow them to be injected with an experimental drug because you were told by deceitful governments and a biased science, that's what should happen 'for the greater good'.

— That despite being informed that children are up to one hundred times more likely to die from the vaccine rather than the virus, you allowed them to be injected anyway.

— That you would ignore the growing data on adverse effects and deaths caused globally by the vaccines, that were outnumbering those of the virus itself (real data as opposed to made up ones).

— That you would refuse to listen to an objective viewpoint by eminent doctors, scientists and lawyers because you were told not to listen to them.

— That you refused to look at contrary information to the ones fed to you by one source, despite that source being proven to be unscrupulous, deceitful and not following their own rules.

— That you did not ask why the mainstream media does not cover vaccine related deaths or injuries, or the many protests and gatherings around the world. When over a million people turn up to protest for freedom in a major city in the world, you don't ask why the media don't show it.

— That you don't ask why the suspicious deaths of presidents, rulers and top CEO's that offered a dissenting voice, are not given investigative journalism coverage by the worldwide press?

— That despite the cries of those opposing the loss of freedom, you did not say *no* to the vaccine passport.

— That you will not say *no* to the ID chip being inserted inside you.

— That you stopped asking why?

Why have you stopped asking why? It is not too late. There is still time. The train can still be stopped. Are you ready to get off that train and fight for the freedom of humanity?

We bloody hope so. For your sake, ours, for our children, for future generations and for the survival of humanity.

#MOCKINGJAY: Part 4 The Message

Sofia made her way down the hill past the warning signs of 'Private Property' and 'KEEP OUT'. She ignored all warning signs both externally and internally. Her heart threatened to leap from the cage in her chest and run as far from the rest of her as possible. She breathed in deeply regularly, to reassure both her heart and herself that she was exactly where she was meant to be.

Blackened like a panther stalking its prey, Sofia slinked through the grass of the forest, silent and stealth like as Marcus had taught her during training. He had seen what was ahead long before she had heard the whispers. A chance meeting, a hidden fascination and she was hooked into his own mission — to prepare himself and others for the greatest challenge facing humanity.

As she made her way through the trees and the long grass towards her destination and perhaps her destiny, she felt the fear and trepidation threaten to crush her. Despite her outward soldierly appearance, at that moment she questioned both her ability and capacity for fulfilling this assignment.

'When the moment arises, know you have been chosen. You and only you will be given that mission. And whatever you choose to do, whatever choice you make, honour it and be grateful for it. Whether you choose to fulfil it or not, is irrelevant; free choice and the retainment of free will, is your hero. That is what we are striving for against a movement set on stealing it. There will be no right or wrong choice; simply your right to choose.'

Marcus's words repeated in her head and ensured she kept moving forward. Her heart let go of the cage and sat back and calmed itself down.

'I don't have to do this,' she whispered to herself, 'I choose to. For myself and for the good of man. No ...' She stopped for a moment and gripped her hands firmly around the weapons she carried — a black baton and a long knife, then she set her jaw and tightened her mouth, '... for the survival of man!'

She continued her journey as midnight approached. She listened to the night owls and the various crickets and cicadas that filled the air around her with their music. Although isolated in her everyday life, she was aware that she was never truly alone. She had a life online with likeminded and awakened souls and of course, her cat and the animals and insects of the nearby forest.

During the three hour car journey to this destination, she played music to lift her soul — Latin dance music and the Gypsy Kings were her favorites. Music she had spent many a drunken night dancing to across the border with Mexican friends. Then there were the tracks from Queen that she found herself singing along to and pop songs from the '80s. Banished were the soulful tunes of her regular playlist.

After more than half an hour of walking through dense forest, with just her compass for direction and instructions in her ears, she found the open grassland that lay below the hill to the compound; the place where her purpose lay. This was the bit she was dreading most of all. Sensor lights were set at a particular height so it was imperative she kept below that to ensure she did not trigger alarms and jeopardise both herself and the mission. She was going to have to crouch low and run in a lowered position. It was a long way down and she was no soldier. She had been lifting weights and doing hundreds of squats in preparation, but she knew that it was still going to be a challenge for her. The alternative was to crawl on her belly, like the snakes she dreaded she might meet along the way.

She took her chances with the crouch. With stealth and determination, she made her way down the hill ignoring the growing aches in her thighs. Halfway down, she felt the tears welling as the dull ache became more and more screamingly painful. She wanted so much to stand up and stretch them out, but that was not an option. Instead, she was forced to lie on her back and stretch them that way. She felt the pain of the release of built up blood rushing through her lower limbs. All the while, her thoughts were around her as she listened for a slithery or hissing sound. As soon as she was able, she resumed her crouch run, but found that she had to repeat the stretch out back against the ground position twice more. Each time her heart sat shivering for comfort in her mouth.

Finally, after forty minutes of her decent and rest procedure, she arrived at the fence. As instructed by

Marcus, she used the speciality wire cutters and ensured the thickened rubber gloves he had sent her in the post, were positioned firmly on her hands before she attempted the cutting. Warning signs of electrocution stood around the fence perimeter like silent execution guards.

In minutes, she had cut a hole large enough to fit herself through. Marcus had also taught her how to make herself smaller than her body mass. It was a specialist technique and she had learned it painfully on a smaller mission not dissimilar to this one; albeit that was merely a training mission and the voltage a fraction of this, which thankfully was switched off or to a lower voltage.

A camera was attached to her collar bone to enable Marcus visual access to her progress. This enabled him to instruct her through the ear piece she wore. She fixed the fence as she was taught and was about to move forward.

'Wait!' he cried out. She stood still, silent and without breath. There was a movement to her left.

'Run to the wall on the right and hide into the crack opening,' he instructed. She did as she was told and squeezed herself as much as she could into inches of an opening in the wall. He had taught her well. The guard did not see her.

'There's a door around the side of that wall. It will be locked. Use the 'special key'. *Ah, finally, that key* she thought with nervous excitement. She found the door and extracted the key from one of her many pockets filled with gadgets, tools and weapons. She had already ditched the baton and knife beside a formidable tree before entering the long grass and her descent down the hill. Those weapons were for animals and perhaps the odd guard unaccounted for.

The special key opened the door. She didn't ask how or why, but simply breathed out a sigh of relief and gratitude.

Next she was instructed to shoot out the lights with a tiny silencer gun she kept in her backpack for this exact purpose. When all the lights were out, she put on her night vision glasses; normal looking glasses with a yellow lens. Another of Marcus' finds. He instructed her movements and although her heart still occasionally banged on its cage, she found herself feeling more and more calm. Perhaps it was knowing that Marcus was with her every step of the way and knowing he had her back, that appeased her fears. Or perhaps it was a feeling of empowerment and self-pride, that she, a marketing manager with a passion for books, had been chosen out of all the billions of people on the planet, to fulfil this one mission.

A mission of spectacular importance; a plan to wake up the world.

She was amazed that she passed very few guards. Marcus told her that he worked at this place many years ago and that he knew it 'like the back of my hand' he said. Indeed he did, for the hidden corners and nooks and crannies of the building was where he led her.

'Okay, this is it. This is the door. Be careful. I don't know what lies behind.'

'Oh great!' she whispered in shock. Now her mind was alive with all kinds of panic and her heart was doing flips in her chest.

'Stay calm. Breathe. Remember your inner place meditation training. Sofia, find your inner place.' The gentleness of Marcus' words spoke into her and created a safety rope for her to find her way back from fear. She allowed the rope to descend into the depths of her being. There, in the stillness of her soul, like a calm oasis, lay her peace. She centred herself and rebalanced her breathing.

'Good, well done Sofia. You're doing just fine. Now, when you are ready, use the special key again to open the door. And Sofia,' Marcus said with a gentleness she had never heard in his voice before, 'no matter what happens from now on in, you will always be my hero.' She smiled as she placed the key in the door and steadied herself.

The room was dark and smelled of old dust. It was exactly as Marcus described it to her. She could hear him sigh with relief in her ear.

'It's exactly how I had left it,' he declared. 'Now remember what I told you? How to fire it up and what to do? You will have exactly twenty minutes from the time the system is live and you press the enter key, to getting back onto the top of the hill, do you understand?'

'Yes.'

'Okay Sofia, let's do this.'

For the next half hour, the two of them worked together to re-construct a communications system that could override every visual media platform in the world by renegotiating a signal to each satellite above earth. Despite him explaining it to her, it was way too technical for Sofia's mind to comprehend. She simply trusted that Marcus knew what he was doing. She had never told him how attracted to him she was, especially since she was still recovering from the break-up with Billy when they met, but also because he was such a serious and focused individual. She intuitively knew that her attraction feelings were to remain undisclosed unless initiated by him. She was however, in these crucial moments of her life, completely connected to him and that comforted her as her hands did as he instructed her to make them do.

'Okay, it's ready. Are you ready Sofia? You can still back out. Nobody will judge you. There is still time to back out of this.'

Sofia thought for a moment. He was right, she could still walk away. Twenty minutes to exit the building, find the hole in the fence, unhook it, exit without becoming fried bread, crouch run up a hill to avoid triggering the sensors, finding the weapons again in case she required defending herself and then getting back to the truck and driving off. Twenty minutes was a quarter of the time she required to do all that. Yet as she flicked on the green light switch and entered the words into the computer and then pressed enter, she knew, that despite the outcome, this wasn't about her. Life wasn't about her. She had to prove her existence by living, yes, but life was about others. If her life ended tonight after accomplishing the mission, she knew she had truly lived a purposeful life.

When Sofia finally awoke, it took her a while to acknowledge her surroundings. She felt the ache in her body before she saw the light pour through the cracks of the curtains. She tried to get up but her back and legs were as heavy as lead. She took a moment to focus and then to reflect. Her mind was empty and there were no thoughts save her environment and the pains in her body. She breathed. In with the breath, out with the breath. Words from meditations flooded back to her consciousness. She took in those waking moments to breathe and to give thanks for that breath. Then she smiled. A slow, self-appreciative smile. It was met with the long, Southern drawl of her purring cat Archie.

'Hey you,' she offered as she lifted her hand to stroke him. She saw the cuts and scratches along her arms and felt them on her legs. Then she remembered.

After she pressed enter, Marcus shouted,

'now get out of there Sofia and run!' She did not stop running. She did not trigger sensor lights or the guards who suspected nothing from a deserted, old military communications centre due for demolition in the coming months.

She ran as though her life depended on it and nothing was going to stand in her way, not even the branches of the trees.

'Okay, okay, I'm awake. I'm up!' she cried out to the demanding cat. 'I'm up!,' she said as she winced with each sitting up movement. She felt every muscle in her back that had allowed her to be a superhero for one night. But now she was suffering the physical depletion. Coffee was her kryptonite; copious amounts of fresh, ground coffee.

She made her way to the kitchen, filled up the coffee machine, switched it on and checked her phone. Countless messages from Marcus to call him.

'Hey Marcus. Just got up. Sorry I missed your calls. All okay?'

'Man Sofia, where you been?'

'Sleeping! What time is it anyhow?' she asked as she squinted at the kitchen clock. 'Shoot! It's almost one in the afternoon! I can't believe I slept for so long!'

'Sofia,' Marcus cut in.

'Yes?'

'You did it! You bloody did it!' Then she remembered last night. It came flooding back to her.

'I did?' she asked.

'I'm so proud of you Sofia. You are truly the most amazing soul.'

Sofia smiled. And something else was triggered by the kindness of his voice: an old memory, a desire long hidden, a sense of wanting.

'Do you want to know exactly what you did Sofia?' Marcus interrupted her thoughts.

'Something to do with what I wrote into the computer screen right?'

'Yes. But those words you wrote, do you know where they went after you pressed enter?'

She shook her head but realised he couldn't see her.

'No, I haven't a clue. I guessed into a system somewhere?' she heard Marcus laugh.

'I bloody love you girl. You are unbelievable!' His South African accent, normally curt and authoritative from years of military existence, was soft and warm. She smiled again. 'You got a TV?'

'You know I do but I only use it for watching films. I can't bear it other than that.'

'Switch it on. Now.' Taken aback, she did as she was instructed. She didn't question Marcus such was the impact of his training on her. It took a while to change batteries in the TV remote since it had not been used for terrestrial television channels since she had arrived.

'Which channel?' she asked absently. She heard him laugh.

'It doesn't matter. Just choose one.'

Although she thought that was an odd statement, she did as she was asked and randomly flicked on channel one. She stood there agape as she read the message. Then she tried another channel and another. All the channels held the same message. The one Marcus instructed her to type into that computer the night before. Tears welled up and then fell onto her face and down her neck. She was sobbing.

'We did it Sofia. We did it.' Marcus repeated softly as he allowed her sobs to fill up the conversation. 'You are amazing. I am so proud of you. Humanity will have to stop and wake up now. Because of your bravery Sofia; because of you, many lives could be saved. You truly are a beautiful soul.'

And as she listened to Marcus, repeating comforting words of encouragement and accomplishment, the tears continued to fall. But her eyes did not leave the screen as she read the words that billions of people were reading on their televisions, computer and phone screens at the same time. It took them until late afternoon before they could switch off the message that Sofia and Marcus had given to the world and by then, it was all the world was talking about.

— YOU ARE A SOVERIGN HUMAN BEING
— YOU HAVE INALIENABLE RIGHTS
— NOBODY HAS THE POWER TO CONTROL YOU
  EXCEPT YOU
— THERE IS AN EVIL DICTATORSHIP CONTROLING

YOU AND IS NOW TRYING TO DESTROY YOU
AND THOSE AROUND YOU
— WAKE UP AND STOP THEM!
— AND REMEMBER THIS
— LOVE CONQUERS ALL

AND FINALLY ...

It's not too late. You can say *no* to allowing the children to be injected. You can say *no* to the boosters, no to the vaccine passports, *no* to the ID chips, not to the discrimination and segregation in society. *No* to the persecution of those who are unjabbed. After all, if you miss just one booster shot, you are then classed as unvaccinated.

We can all work together to demand justice, to create our own events, our own media information and to disseminate truth and refute the propaganda of fear that has presided over our lives for almost two years. It is not too late to ask the questions ...

— What is in the injections?

— Why is there no list of ingredients and side effects?

— Why are the CDC, Fauci, NIAID, the W.H.O., the Gates Foundation, the vaccine pharmaceuticals, the media, the courts, the judicial system all in cahoots together?

— Who is telling the truth?

—Why have they silenced so many people; some permanently?

— And importantly ... if this is all true and there is a global conspiracy to destroy humanity and the world we know, then why and who is behind this?

ASK THE QUESTIONS you didn't ask before. We will win. We won't let them destroy us.

And if you do not believe any of what is written in this book, then that is entirely your choice. We may be right, we may be wrong — that depends on your perspective of the world. Remember, that the greatest gift we possess, is one of free will.

Though if your world has been rocked by these revelations, stay strong. Don't quit; don't give up. We need you and we need each other.

Have hope, look to your Creator for help and trust in the goodness and kindness that still exists in much of humanity. And remember to stay in the light because only light will chase away the shadows of encroaching darkness. And always, always remember, that ...

LOVE CONQUERS ALL!

Learn from yesterday, live for today, hope for tomorrow. The important thing is not to stop questioning.

Albert Einstein

Suggestions to Build Your Immune System and Help Restore Your Body

* Research all below and check doses. You may be allergic to some of these ingredients. You know your body. These are helpful suggestions for you to help build your immune system whether you are jabbed or not. It is time to be the best we can be. It is time to fight back and reclaim our health.

1. Drink White pine needle tea, dandelion tea, fennel and/or Star Anise tea — they all have shikimic acid which possess cancer fighting, antiviral, antimicrobial, anticoagulant and antithrombotic properties. Also known to help neutralise the spike protein. Wheatgrass and wheatgrass juice also have high levels of shikimic acid.

2. Take Quercetin - plays a vital role in health and disease.

3. Take high dose levels of Vitamin D, vitamin C and Zinc. Zinc contributes to wound healing, plus has antioxidant properties and modulates mRNA levels of cytokines.

4. If hospitalised, DON'T go on a ventilator. Up to 80% of patients don't make it on a ventilator. Ask for 10,000 units of intravenous Vitamins C, D and Zinc. Also ask for a drug called Budesonide, a steroid that reduces the inflammation around the lungs. Don't take no for an answer. It isn't protocol for the hospital, but you have patient rights. Fight for the right treatment.

5. Eat crushed garlic - huge medicinal purposes to boost immune system.
6. Bath regularly in Epsom Salts - detoxifies the body.
7. Take C60 or Carbon 60 (1-3 drops per day) - rich source of electrons, promotes healing and reduces inflammation. Also called a 'free radical sponge'. More powerful than most antioxidants.
8. PQQ Pyrroloquinoline quinone/ methoxatin. Found in many fruits and vegetable. And also found in breast milk. Powerful antioxidant fighting toxins and free radicals. Supports energy and generates mitochondria - these are organelles found in the cells of every complex organisms. Vital in cell survival.
9. Suramin — powerful anti-inflammatory. Also known to reverse autism.
10. Iodine - detoxifies compounds and strongly increases the mRNA decay rate.
11. Taking full spectrum hemp extract — has positive effects on our endocannabinoid system which regulates almost every internal function.
12. Take charcoal capsules. Detoxifier and blood purifier.
13. Eat citrus fruits like blood oranges - high hesperidin content, which may help deactivate the spike protein.
14. Look into the following super herbs which may help to disable the spike protein — Schizandra Berry — St John's Wort — Comfrey

Leaf — Feverfew — Ginko Biloba Leaf — Giant Hyssop or Horsemint — Liquidambar (sweetgum).

15. Keep supplies of Ivermectin and Hydroxychloroquine (HQQ) and use either as a prophylactic or as a treatment at start of Covid symptoms. Visit the website @americasfrontlinedoctors.org for more information. And remember that they have to be prescribed by a doctor and not by a vet! Some countries may not have access to these two drugs.

This is your body, your choice so do the right thing for you.

Freedom is a state of mind.

Love is a state of being.

Live a free and loving life.